key influ

profiles

radical

links

TEAM OBAMA

All The President's *Real* Men And Women

Grassfire Nation

Printed in the United States of America

First Printing, 2012

ISBN 0-9849860-2-6

Grassfire Nation
PO Box 277
Maxwell, IA 50161

www.Grassfire.com

About Grassfire Nation

Grassfire Nation, a division of Grassroots Action,
Inc., is a million-strong network of grassroots
conservatives dedicated to equipping you with the
tools that give you a real impact on the key issues of
our day. We also operate a social networking site
(PatriotActionNetwork.com) and a patriot-sourced
news website (LibertyNews.com).

Table of Contents

Team Obama

Introduction
Who is Barack Obama?

Four years into his Presidency, we still don't know who he is.

The truth about Barack Obama—his past and politics—is something most in the mainstream media shied away from during the 2008 presidential election. Yes, they covered his speeches and policies, and gave light treatment to his time in the Illinois legislature and the U.S. Senate. But that was nothing like the intense investigation to which John McCain's vice-presidential pick, Sarah Palin, was treated. Teams of reporters descended on Wasilla, Alaska, in search of details about the conservative firebrand and the *New York Times* called on readers to help sift through Palin's email correspondence. We learned about the church she attended and tried to find out whether she had spoken in tongues.

For Barack Obama, it was a different story—or in most cases, no story at all. When it came to the life and times of Barack Obama, journalists showed themselves decidedly incurious about the details of his upbringing and the many troubling connections in his past.

The result is that, in many ways, Barack Obama remains a mystery to the American public.

A man is known by the company he keeps. And in the case of Barack Hussein Obama, that company has been almost exclusively on the left—the hard left. So we've set out in *Team Obama* to introduce you to the men and women to whom Obama has been linked by birth and by choice. It's an amazing collection of liberals, leftists, radicals, and, yes, communists.

Radical scholar Manning Marable revealed the truth when he wrote, *after* Obama's presidential election, that:

> What makes Obama different is that he has also been a community organiser. He has read left literature, including my works, and *he understands what socialism is.* A lot of the people working with him are, indeed, socialists with backgrounds in the Communist Party or as independent Marxists. There are a lot of people like that in Chicago who have worked with him for years. [1]

Too bad we didn't know that beforehand. Yes, we learned a bit about Jeremiah Wright and Bill Ayers during the campaign, but not much. Media accounts then and since failed to probe the deep links Obama has with both men. As a result, Obama was able to safely distance himself from the loquacious and venomous Wright and pass off unrepentant domestic terrorist and self-described small "c" communist Bill Ayers as just a "guy who lives in my neighborhood...who I know."

But it's not just Wright and Ayers that offer telling clues to the real Obama. There is a network of leftists, socialists and communists surrounding him that is much wider and deeper than just those two.

Even his long-time Chicago doctor is a leftist.

David Scheiner, M.D., treated Barack Obama from 1987 until he entered the White House. Like so many in the long trail of friends, colleagues, and political associates in Obama's youth and adulthood, Scheiner has impeccable credentials as a lefty.

An internist based in Chicago's Hyde Park neighborhood, Scheiner belongs to Physicians for a National Health Program, a far-left group focused on single-payer national health care or, as Dr. Scheiner put it to author Edward Klein, "socialized medicine." [2]

Going into Obama's first term, Scheiner had high hopes that his former patient would give the nation socialized health care. He told Klein that Obama told him he favored government-controlled medicine as practiced in Canada and Western Europe.

But even though ObamaCare puts American health care under government control and places us on a glide path toward a single-payer system, that's not good enough for Scheiner. He knocks Obama for not giving the nation "Medicare for all." [3]

Scheiner, who has treated other Hyde Park patients and partisans like former U.S. Sen. Carol Moseley-Braun and the late Studs Terkel, practiced medicine in partnership with Dr. Quentin Young, a man with even more highly burnished left-wing credentials— and someone who has long been an Obama ally and confidant.

Young is a Chicago socialist who was identified as a member of the Communist Party USA before a congressional committee in 1968. He took the Fifth Amendment when asked about his membership. [4]

He is also the founder of Physicians for a National Health Program and a long-time advocate of single-payer medicine, aka socialized health care. Young, along with John McKnight, one of Obama's mentors in community organizing, founded the Health and Medicine Policy Research Group, also a strong backer of government-controlled health care.

Along with other Chicago radicals, Young was in the home of former Weatherman Underground leader Bill Ayers in 1995 when state senator Alice Palmer, a communist sympathizer, announced her plan to run for Congress and named Obama as her successor.

As to the relationship between Ayers' and Obama, Young said they were "friends." [5] Yes, and so much more as we shall see.

Scheiner, Young, McKnight, Palmer, Ayers and Wright. All radicals. All friends of Obama. And we're just getting started in detailing the thick network of leftists, radicals, socialists and communists that pop up at every stage in the life of America's 44th president.

Researcher Stanley Kurtz, author of *Radical-in-Chief,* and the leading sleuth into Obama's socialist past, says there is "a continuous ideological trail, ranging from the childhood influence of Obama's radical mentor, Frank Marshall Davis, to the Socialist Scholars Conferences of Obama's New York years, to the future president's community organizing days and political career." [6]

The upshot of all these friends, allies, associates, and influences?

As Kurtz tells it, "Evidence clearly indicates that the President of the United States is a socialist." [7]

Team Obama

Gulp.

Team Obama presents the names and, in at least one case, the Communist Party membership number, of the men and women of the Left who walked with Obama in his past and present.

Let's start at the very beginning.

1

Like Father, Like Son

Barack Obama, Sr.

I t is safe to say that Barack Obama's upbringing was anything but traditional. The son of an absentee father from Kenya and a free-spirited mother, Obama spent his childhood in Hawaii and Indonesia, raised by his young mother and her second husband, and then, after age 10, in the home of his grandparents in Honolulu. His father, Barack Obama, Sr., left Hawaii in 1963 to study at Harvard, after which Obama saw him just once, in 1971, for about a month.

Despite his dad's modest personal investment in his life, his father's "heritage was to be a major influence on his world view, ideals and priorities," according to the *Boston Globe*, which reported in 1990 that Obama began regular correspondence with his father while in high school.[8]

Obama told the world just how influential his absent father was in his 1995 political coming-of-age memoir *Dreams from My Father*. In it, he recalled how his mother repeatedly cited his father's "distant authority" in her effort to shape her young son's character and identity. She told him about elder Obama's hard life growing up "poor, in a poor country, in a poor continent" and that "he was diligent and honest, no matter what it cost him."

That gilded memory involved some serious stretching of the truth. As Obama later learned, his father had not been altogether honest with his mother, failing to tell her that he had another wife back in Africa and later abandoning her when we went to Harvard to pursue a Ph.D. in economics. Whatever his father's failings, "I would follow his example, my mother decided. I had no choice. It was in the genes."[9]

In his fascinating decoding of the Obama enigma, *The Roots of Obama's Rage*, author Dinesh D'Souza presents the father as the key to understanding the son. Handsome, with a deep baritone voice that carried a British accent, Obama, Sr., was an undeniably charismatic and highly intelligent man. He was also deeply flawed. With a taste for strong drink and for women, he was often inebriated and unable to keep himself steadily employed. He fathered eight children by four women and died in 1982 in a drunk-driving accident.

Still, as D'Souza writes, Obama's mother "cultivated in her son Barack, Jr., an almost mystical reverence for his absentee father."[10] The mission of Obama's life, says D'Souza, is to fulfill the dreams he inherited from his father. And he's not alone in saying so. As Sarah Obama, one of the wives of Obama's grandfather, told *Newsweek*, "I look at him and I see all the same things—he has taken everything from his father. The son is realizing everything the father wanted. The dreams of the father are still alive in the son."[11]

Obama bears testimony, as well, to the central role of his father in defining his life purpose. He calls *Dreams from My Father* "the record of a personal, interior journey—a boy's search for his father and through that search a workable meaning for his life as a black American."[12]

So what are the father's "dreams" that the son has been seeking to fulfill over the past four years, an almost nightmarish time of troubles marked by sluggish economic growth, rising unemployment, and record-breaking federal spending?

The ideological "dream" that animated Obama, Sr., was anti-colonialism, an outlook hostile to the developed world and one widely shared by elites in nations such as Kenya which gained independence from Britain in 1963. Anti-colonialists "were anti-Western and oriented toward national self-determination, but their ideology also contained noticeable strains of Marxism and socialism," writes D'Souza.

The earmarks of anti-colonialism, D'Souza observes, include the beliefs that colonial empires are founded in violence, are racist, steal the subordinated nation's wealth, are led nowadays by the United States, and will not end unless the colonizers are forced out.

All this, D'Souza argues, constitutes a worldview embraced by Obama: "From a very young age and throughout his formative years, Obama learned to see America as a force for global domination and destruction."[13] With his father as guide, he also "grew to perceive the rich as an oppressive class, a kind of neocolonial power within America."[14]

The elder Obama's economic views are revealed in his 1965 paper, "Problems Facing Our Socialism," published in the *East Africa Journal*. In it, Obama calls communal land ownership "one of the best African traditions," favors nationalizing foreign owned firms, says the government has a role in forcing private firms to employ Africans for key roles, and says it is the "government's obligation" to "find means by which we can redistribute our economic gains to the benefit of all."

Obama, Sr., also declares that "the government should tax the rich more so as to generate high tax surpluses" and he toys with the idea of 100 percent taxation:

> Theoretically, there is nothing that can stop the government from taxing 100 percent of income so long as the people get benefits from the government commensurate with their income which is taxed.... I do not see why the government cannot tax those who have more and syphon some of these revenues into savings which can be utilized in investment for future development....[15]

It sounds all too familiar. While the son might not say it with the same candor, it's clear from his unguarded exchange with "Joe the Plumber," his rhetorical bludgeoning of "fat cats" on Wall Street, and his relentless effort to raise taxes on "the rich" that father and son share a common dream.

By means of an "incredible osmosis," the father "was able to transmit his ideology to his son living in America," writes D'Souza. The "father's dream has become his dream. It is a dream that, as President, he is imposing with a vengeance on America and the world."[16]

But however outsized and fundamental the role played by his father in formulating Obama's outlook on life, his mother played a lead role as well. Meet Stanley Ann Dunham.

2

An "Intellectual Rebel"

Stanley Ann Dunham: Mother, Unitarian Socialist

Barack Obama, Sr.'s, starring role in setting the ideological course of Obama's life from a continent away came in large part because of Obama, Jr.'s, mother, Stanley Ann Dunham, "the dominant figure in my formative years," Obama said in an interview. "The values she taught me continue to be my touchstone when it comes to how I go about the world of politics."[17] She was, Obama wrote, a "lonely witness for secular humanism, a soldier for New Deal, Peace Corps, position-paper liberalism."[18]

Ann Dunham was an 18-year-old University of Hawaii student when she gave birth to Barack Obama in 1961. She divorced his father, Barack Obama, Sr., in 1964 and married Indonesian Lolo Soetoro two years later. She later earned a Ph.D. in anthropology, but died in 1995, at age 52 from ovarian cancer.

An "intellectual rebel," who blossomed during her teen years on Mercer Island, just outside Seattle, Dunham had a "fledgling beatnik sensibility that would eventually take her around the globe," according to a *Seattle Times* report that featured the recollections of high school classmates.

"She touted herself as an atheist, and it was something she'd read about and could argue," said Dunham's high school best friend, Maxine Box. "She was always challenging and arguing and comparing. She was already thinking about things that the rest of us hadn't."

One teacher, Jim Wichterman, who included Karl Marx and "The Communist Manifesto" in his philosophy course, still had a sharp memory of Dunham 47 years after she graduated.

"As much as a high-school student can, she'd question anything: What's so good about democracy? What's so good about capitalism? What's wrong with communism? What's good about communism? She had what I call an inquiring mind." [19]

Those were questions John Stenhouse, chairman of the Mercer Island School Board, could have answered quite well. He testified in 1955 before the House Un-American Activities Subcommittee that he had been a member of the Communist Party.

The classroom instruction of Wichterman and another teacher, Val Foubert , who assigned readings from Margaret Mead on homosexuality, prompted parental outrage and calls for the two teachers' dismissal. Ann's parents, Stanley and Madalyn Dunham did not join the protest.

They had already dispensed with the doctrinal confines of their Baptist and Methodist backgrounds and were attending East Shore Unitarian Church, a congregation that offered a great deal more theological and political latitude. Some called it "The Little Red Church on the Hill." [20] It was a place, the *Chicago Tribune* reported, where the kind of skepticism Stanley practiced and passed on to his daughter Ann was welcomed. [21]

Later, in Hawaii, Obama's grandfather or grandmother took him as a young boy to the First Unitarian Church of Honolulu—a hyper-liberal congregation that offered sanctuary to military deserters during the Vietnam War. The church celebrated 50 years of existence in 2003 with T-shirts declaring "Liberal Religion for 50 Years." The *Honolulu Star-Bulletin* filled in the picture:

> Activism for peace and human rights causes has characterized the congregation of the First Unitarian Church of Honolulu since it was organized 50 years ago. Members were instrumental in founding the League of Women Voters and activating a local branch of the American Civil Liberties Union. It offered sanctuary to servicemen who went AWOL to avoid being sent to Vietnam. It helped launch the Save Our Constitution effort to fight the constitutional amendment on same-sex marriages....

> After leaving Hawaii to work at the Unitarian seminary in Berkeley, Calif., (Church co-founder Rosemary) Mattson and her husband were active in the international peace movement. She escorted more than 25 tours of Americans to the former Soviet Union for people-to-people experience. [22]

The church was the site of Madelyn Dunham's memorial service in 2008.

The Dunham's links to left-wing Unitarian churches in Washington and Hawaii fits with

Obama's description of his grandfather as someone who "had come to consider himself as something of a freethinker—bohemian, even. That outlook, transmitted to daughter and to the grandson he helped raise, led him to "enroll the family in the local Unitarian Universalist congregation; he liked the idea that Unitarians drew on the scriptures of all the great religions ('It's like you get five religions in one,' he would say)." [23]

And that freethinking attitude led Stanley Dunham to strike up a relationship with black journalist and Communist Party member Frank Marshall Davis, a Stalinist on whom the FBI compiled a book-length file. This man became a friend and counselor to young Barack.

3

"A Poet Named Frank"

Frank Marshall Davis, Communist Mentor

B arack Obama gently introduces readers to a man he calls "Frank" in his 1995 memoir, *Dreams from My Father*. Frank, we're told, in Obama's circumspect version, was an elderly gentleman who "had enjoyed some modest notoriety once, [and] was a contemporary of writer Richard Wright and poet and playwright Langston Hughes during his years in Chicago." [24] Wright was a Communist Party member who gave up his party membership in 1942; Hughes was a communist sympathizer and admirer of Stalin.

What we're not told in Obama's lyrical and factually deficient account of his early life is that Frank, his adolescent counselor, was Frank Marshall Davis, a man whose Communist Party membership and engagement with a long list of communist front groups generated a 601-page FBI file over 19 years of surveillance. And a man who denounced author Richard Wright for exposing the party in the classic work, *The God That Failed*—something Davis blasted as an "act of treason." [25]

Davis' communist involvement may date as far back as 1931, but he was definitely linked to numerous Communist front groups in the late 1930s, including the National Negro Congress, the League of American

Writers, the National Federation for Constitutional Liberties, and the Civil Rights Congress. [26]

He joined the Communist Party USA in 1943 while working in Chicago as managing editor and, later, executive editor of the *Associated Negro Press*, a news service for black newspapers. At a time when millions had already perished under Soviet communism, Davis celebrated the land of Lenin and Stalin, writing in 1947:

> I admire Russia for wiping out an economic system which permitted a handful of rich to exploit and beat gold from the millions of plain people.... As one who believes in freedom and democracy for all, I honor the Red nation.

Davis, whose Communist Party USA card number was 47544, moved to Hawaii in 1948 with his second wife, Helen Canfield Davis, also a Communist Party member (CP # 62109). They made the move at the suggestion of Davis' friend Paul Robeson, an American celebrity and Communist Party member who was star-struck by Stalin. After visiting Russia, Robeson offered a glowing report of life in the worker's paradise, even defending Stalin's purges. "From what I have already seen of the workings of the Soviet Government," Robeson said, "I can only say that anybody who lifts his hand against it ought to be shot!" [27]

Once in Hawaii, Davis began writing a column, "Frankly Speaking," for a recently launched communist weekly newspaper. Historian Paul Kengor has reviewed those half-century old columns and writes that they "flawlessly parroted official Soviet propaganda."

Davis also found time in the Aloha state to take pictures of the Hawaii coastline, using a camera with a telescopic lens, according to the FBI. Hawaii's status as a mid-Pacific outpost of U.S. military power made it of great importance to the Communist Party USA and its minders in Moscow. The FBI report states that:

> Informant stated that DAVIS spent much of his time in this activity. He said this was the third different occasion DAVIS had been observed photographing shorelines and beachfronts. Informant advised that it did not appear he was photographing any particular objects. [28]

This "poet" and man of "modest notoriety" became a counselor to Obama during his formative adolescent years. As Kengor writes, "a mentor of the current president of the United States was a Communist — and not only a party member, but an actual propagandist for Stalin's USSR...."

The influence of Davis on Obama was not inconsequential. In his new book, *The Communist — Frank Marshall Davis: The Untold Story of Barack Obama's Mentor*, Kengor notes that Obama devotes 2,500 words in *Dreams* to Davis, who "surfaces repeatedly from start to finish, from Hawaii to Los Angeles to Chicago to Germany to Kenya ... from the 1970s to the 1980s to the 1990s." [29]

Obama's grandfather, Stanley Dunham, introduced Obama to Davis in 1970, according to Dawna Weatherly-Williams, a friend of the two men. At the time, Davis already "knew Stan real well," Weatherly-Williams told the *Telegraph* newspaper. "They'd play Scrabble and drink and crack jokes and argue."

"Stan had been promising to bring Barry by because

we all had that in common—Frank's kids were half-white, Stan's grandson was half-black and my son was half-black. We all had that in common and we all really enjoyed it. We got a real kick out of reality." [30]

Maya Soetoro-Ng, Obama's half-sister, said her grandfather saw Davis as "a point of connection, a bridge if you will, to the larger African-American experience for my brother." [31]

Obama relates two occasions when the elderly man shared his "hard-earned knowledge" with young Barack. After a confrontation erupted between his grandparents over his grandmother's fear of a black panhandler—something Stanley Dunham thought rooted in racism—teen Obama made his way over to Frank's house to sort it all out.

After sharing whiskey together, Davis delivered an oracle about the fixity of the racial divide—and the legitimacy of black hate. "What I'm trying to tell you is, your grandma's right to be scared," Davis says. "...She understands that black people have a reason to hate. That's just how it is. For your sake, I wish it were otherwise. But it's not. So you might as well get used to it." [32]

At their last get together, just before Obama left for Occidental College in Los Angeles, Davis warned Obama not to abandon his race by letting college turn him into a "well-trained, well-paid nigger." [33]

"Understand something, boy," Davis told Obama. "You're not going to college to get educated. You're going there to get trained. They'll train you to want what you don't need. They'll train you to manipulate words so they don't mean anything anymore. They'll train you to forget what it is that you already know.

They'll train you so good, you'll start believing what they tell you about equal opportunity and the American way and all that shit." [34]

Obama took those words to heart. "To avoid being mistaken for a sellout, I chose my friends carefully," Obama writes in *Dreams*. "The more politically active black students. The foreign students. The Chicanos. The Marxist professors and structural feminists and punk-rock performance poets. We smoked cigarettes and wore leather jackets. At night, in the dorms, we discussed neocolonialism, Franz Fanon, Eurocentrism, and patriarchy." [35]

Guided by Frank, Obama determined not to let college compromise his principles. It's now very clear that he more than succeeded.

4

"Ardent Marxist" in 1980

John Drew and the College Years

The story of Obama's college days, like much else that threatens to unveil the truth about who he is, is still largely in the shadows. He attended Occidental College in Los Angeles from 1979-81 and transferred to Columbia University in New York after his sophomore year, graduating in 1983.

Obama has kept his college transcripts under wraps and rejected media requests to detail his life at Columbia. The *New York Times* reported in 2007 that Obama "declined repeated requests to talk about his New York years, release his Columbia transcript or identify even a single fellow student, co-worker, roommate or friend from those years." [36]

While not much is known about his time at Columbia, at least one Occidental graduate has stepped forward with a striking account of young Barry's well-developed Marxist worldview as a sophomore at the small, prestigious liberal arts school.

"Obama was already an ardent Marxist when I met him in the fall of 1980," claims John C. Drew, Ph.D., who met Obama while visiting his girlfriend at Occidental. "I know it's incendiary to say this," he told author Paul Kengor, but Obama "was basically a Marxist-Leninist." [37]

Then pursuing graduate studies at Cornell, Drew was a 1979 Occidental graduate and a Marxist who in 1976 started what became the Democratic Student Socialist Alliance at Occidental.

His then-girlfriend, Caroline Boss, a committed Marxist, DSA member, and anti-apartheid activist, told Drew, when he visited her around Christmas 1980, that Obama and his roommate Mohammed Hasan Chandoo were "on our side." Drew remembers Boss telling Obama, "You've worked with us.... You've been at our DSA meetings. You've been active in the anti-apartheid movement."

A few days after Christmas 1980 Drew joined his girlfriend, her parents, Obama, and Chandoo at a restaurant where the talk turned to politics. Drew remembers Obama's emphatic assertion that revolution was imminent and inevitable. "Obama repeatedly used the phrase, 'When the revolution comes...,'" Drew writes. "'There's going to be a revolution,' Obama said, 'we need to be organized and grow the movement.' In Obama's view, our role must be to educate others so that we might usher in more quickly this inevitable revolution." [38]

Obama himself testifies to his growing political engagement, writing in *Dreams* that he began, by his sophomore year, to protest apartheid in South Africa and joined the call for corporations to divest from South Africa:

> It had started as something of a lark, I suppose, part of the radical pose my friends and I sought to maintain, a subconscious end run around issues closer to home. But as the months passed and I found myself drawn into a larger role—contacting representatives of the African National Congress to speak on

campus, drafting letters to the faculty, printing up flyers, arguing strategy—I noticed that people had begun to listen to my opinions. [39]

Obama shared his opinions in his maiden political speech, a two-minute affair that ended abruptly with a bit of contrived political theater as two white students tackled Obama and hustled him off-stage—a hamhanded demonstration of white racism in South Africa. That first speech took place at a divestment rally put on by Students for Economic Democracy (SED), a group founded by former student radical Tom Hayden which favored public ownership and control of the economy. While no evidence has been found to show Obama joined SED, his close involvement in the disinvestment campaign—not to mention his Marxist self-identification when talking with Drew—suggests he agreed and aligned with their goals and knew its members and leaders.

Obama told Occidental's magazine in 2004 that it was his "involvement in the South African divestment movement at Occidental that first set him on his current path. 'I got into politics at Occidental.... I made a conscious decision to go into public policy.'" [40]

While not much is known about Obama's life while at Columbia University from 1981-83, it's clear that his leftward political course did not alter. One telling item that has surfaced from Obama's time at Columbia, what the *New York Times* called a "lost chapter" in Obama's life, is an anti-war article he wrote for a school newspaper on March 10, 1983. In "Breaking the War Mentality," Obama took issue with "the relentless, often silent spread of militarism in the country" and praised a couple of anti-war student groups which "are throwing their weight into shifting America off the dead-end track," of the nation's "distorted national priorities."

Obama signaled in the article that his beef with American society was more fundamental than mere matters of war and peace. "One is forced to wonder," he wrote, "whether disarmament or arms control issues, severed from economic and political issues, might be another instance of focusing on the symptoms of a problem instead of the disease itself." [41]

The "disease," in Obama's view, was America's social and economic injustice, a pathology he wanted to cure with his 1983 decision to become a community organizer. It was, he told friends, the pathway to change: "Change in the White House, where Reagan and his minions were carrying on their dirty deeds. Change in the Congress, compliant and corrupt. Change in the mood of the country, manic and self-absorbed. Change won't come from the top, I would say. Change will come from a mobilized grass roots." [42]

Obama doesn't tell us exactly when in 1983 he decided to become an organizer, but one event that precipitated or confirmed Obama's career choice came in the spring of 1983 when he attended the Cooper Union Socialist Scholars Conference. This confab on the 100th anniversary of the death of Karl Marx, opened with an address from Frances Fox Piven, a leading theorist of community organizing, who praised Marx as a man who "helped people around the globe to struggle to make history."[43] Piven instructed the socialist faithful that "We must stand within the intellectual and political tradition Marx bequeathed." [44]

Obama, it seems clear, took those words to heart, setting his sights on a career in community organizing and finding his way, two years later, to Chicago where he went to work under the tutelage of disciples of the master organizer himself, Saul Alinsky.

5

Agitator Extraordinaire

Saul Alinsky, the Father of Commmunity Organizing

I t is one thing for an Obama critic to spotlight the president's many links to the far-left flank of American politics. It's another when a Marxist academic and self-professed Obamaphile makes the same point, in calm and measure cadences. The late Manning Marable, a professor at Columbia and a man who was at one time "probably the best known black Marxist in the country," according to Marxist intellectual Cornel West, issued this appraisal of Obama and his coterie of Chicago friends: [45]

> What makes Obama different is that he has also been a community organiser. He has read left literature, including my works, and *he understands what socialism is.* A lot of the people working with him are, indeed, socialists with backgrounds in the Communist Party or as independent Marxists. There are a lot of people like that in Chicago who have worked with him for years. [46]

Marable declined to name those people in an interview with Aaron Klein, co-author of *The Manchurian Candidate*, but others have identified the leading lights of the Windy City socialist network that surrounded Obama from his arrival in 1985 as a community organizer.

First on the list is agitator extraordinaire Saul Alinsky.

Saul Alinsky died in 1972 when, as President Obama might say, Obama was only ten years old. But the influence of Alinsky on Obama is profound and lasting. He was trained in the Alinsky method by community organizers who, in some cases, had been taught by the master himself.

Obama was, it seems, a keen student. Alinsky's son, David, enthused over Obama's mastery of his father's method in 2008 after the grandiose Democratic National Convention, replete with Roman columns and a stadium setting:

> All the elements were present: the individual stories told by real people of their situations and hardships, the packed-to-the rafters crowd, the crowd's chanting of key phrases and names, the action on the spot of texting and phoning to show instant support and commitment to jump into the political battle, the rallying selections of music, the setting of the agenda by the power people. The Democratic National Convention had all the elements of the perfectly organized event, Saul Alinsky style.
>
> Barack Obama's training in Chicago by the great community organizers is showing its effectiveness. It is an amazingly powerful format, and the method of my late father always works to get the message out and get the supporters on board. When executed meticulously and thoughtfully, it is a powerful strategy

for initiating change and making it really
happen. Obama learned his lesson well. [47]

Labeled "this country's leading hell-raiser" by *The
Nation* magazine, Saul Alinsky invented community
organizing in the 1930s, launching his community
organizing training institute, the Industrial Areas
Foundation, in 1939 with help from millionaire
Marshall Field. Trained as a sociologist, Alinsky
sought to imitate the work of labor organizers, but
in a community setting. He said the community
organizer's task is to overthrow the existing order.

"[W]e are concerned," Alinsky remarked in *Rules
for Radicals*, "with how to create mass organizations
to seize power and give it to the people.... We are
talking about a mass power organization which will
change the world.... This means revolution." [48]

Reaching that goal meant fomenting discontentment
and rage in order to mobilize people for action. "The
organizer dedicated to changing the life of a particular
community must first rub raw the resentments of
the people of the community; fan the latent hostilities
of many of the people to the point of overt
oppression." [49]

The next step is to mobilize for political power by
pitting people against one another along economic
lines. As Alinsky tells readers of *Rules for Radicals*, his
"primer for realistic radicals," "*The Prince* was written
by Machiavelli for the Haves on how to hold power.
Rules for Radicals is written for the Have-Nots on how
to take it away." [50]

Boycotts, sit-ins, rent strikes and other direct action
methods to confront and/or embarrass the "Haves"
were Alinsky's stock-in-trade. And he wasn't afraid

to employ creative and unconventional methods.

He once threatened a "fart-in" at a Rochester Philharmonic concert in order to get attention for his group's demands. Members of FIGHT (Freedom, Independence (later Integration), God, Honor, Today) were told to eat platefuls of baked beans and attend a concert where, as author Nicholas von Hoffman wrote, "they would sit expelling gaseous vapors with such noisy velocity as to compete with the woodwinds." [51]

Alinsky never brought that tactic to the Windy City, but he did take things a step further, threatening a "piss-in" at Chicago's O'Hare Airport to force the city to discuss his demands. Had the city not agreed to talk, Alinsky would have deployed African Americans to occupy urinals and toilets at the airport to the discomfiture and distress of travelers.

It's worth remembering that Alinsky dedicated *Rules for Radicals* to "the first radical known to man who rebelled against the establishment and did it so effectively that he at least won his own kingdom — Lucifer." [52]

For Alinsky, community organizing is all about creating conflict. "When those prominent in the status quo turn and label you an 'agitator' they are completely correct, for that is, in one word, your function—to agitate to the point of conflict." [53]

Agitation was where Obama excelled, according to Mike Kruglik, one of Obama's neighborhood organizing mentors. Obama was the best student Kruglik ever had, claims journalist Ryan Lizza:

> [Obama] was a natural, the undisputed master of agitation, who could engage a room full of

recruiting targets in a rapid-fire Socratic
dialogue, nudging them to admit that they
were not living up to their own standards....
He could be aggressive and confrontational.
With probing, sometimes personal questions,
he would pinpoint the source of pain in their
lives, tearing down their egos just enough
before dangling a carrot of hope that they
could make things better. [54]

And, as wife Michelle Obama, told the media in
1996, her husband brought the techniques of
community organizing into politics. "Barack is not
a politician first and foremost," she said. "He's a
community activist exploring the viability of politics
to make change." [55]

Team Obama

6
Barack's Community Organizing Mentors

Alinsky never joined the Communist Party USA, nor did he claim the socialist label. He was, however, a revolutionary who incited anger along class lines as a lever to force change. Those who follow his method today likewise largely reject ideological classification, but that doesn't change the fact, says Kurtz, that "Community organizing is a largely socialist profession." Instead of claiming the socialist brand, he writes, "America's community organizers have adopted a deliberately stealthy posture," hiding behind popular movements and posing as "pragmatic problem solvers" even as they advance step-by-step toward a socialist future. "Barack Obama's colleagues and mentors were some of the smartest and most influential stealth-socialist community organizers in the country," writes Kurtz. [56] Let's meet several who mentored America's community-organizer-in-chief.

The South Side Mentor: Jerry Kellman, Bringing Social Justice To Black Churches

Alinsky disciple Jerry Kellman hired Obama in 1985 to reach out to churches on Chicago's south side as part of the Developing Communities Project. Kellman's goal, as executive director of DCP, was to "use the 'social justice' teachings of leftwing Catholicism to bring radical politics to black churches." [57] Kellman hired Obama to get past racial and cultural barriers that kept Kellman and other white organizers from gaining the confidence of black pastors.

A long-time leftist who jokes that he "went to the University of Wisconsin to major in student protesting," [58] Kellman learned community organizing at Alinsky's Industrial Areas Foundation after he arrived in Chicago in 1970. He remains active within Chicago's progressive community and close to Obama, who wrote, "To Jerry, a friend and a mentor," In Kellman's copy of *Dreams from My Father*.

Jodi Kantor, author of The Obamas, recalled in an interview a 2009 White House Christmas party encounter between Obama and Kellman...

> ...*The Obamas* often don't mingle freely - they often just stand behind the rope and reach out to shake hands but he sees Jerry Kellman, his old community organizing boss, and he's so happy to see him he reaches across and pulls him in. And Obama says, *"I'm still organizing."* It was a stunning moment and when [Kellman] told me the story, it had echoes of what Valerie Jarrett had told me once - "The senator still thinks of himself as a community organizer." [59]

Alinsky's "Best Disciple": Gregory Galluzzo, The Ruthless Organizer

When the two were in Iowa in 2006 or 2007, Obama reportedly put an arm around Gregory Galluzzo, a former Jesuit priest and long-time community organizer, and credited him for the speed with which his presidential campaign launched its grass-roots operation. Galluzzo, who played a role in bringing Obama to Chicago in 1985 and served as a mentor for Obama, says Obama's election was "like a son winning an office." [60]

Galluzzo has written that he "met with Barack on a regular basis as he incorporated the Developing Communities Project, as he moved the organization into action and as he developed the leadership structure for the organization. He would write beautiful and brilliant weekly reports about his work and the people he was engaging." [61]

Galluzzo calls himself the "best disciple" of Alinsky, who died in 1972 just after Galluzzo arrived in Chicago. With his wife, Mary Gonzalez, Galluzzo founded in 1980 the United Neighborhood Organization of Chicago (UNO), an "in your face" group that tried to bring community organizing to Chicago's Hispanic neighborhoods. He later led the Gamaliel Foundation, which provides leadership training in community organizing and has established a network of 18 affiliates nationwide.

Stanley Kurtz, author of *Radical-in-Chief*, thinks he knows why Obama didn't identify his organizing mentors by name in *Dreams,* using the pseudonym Marty Kaufmann for Jerry Kellman and obscuring the role played by Galluzzo, "once the head of the most aggressive and controversial community organization in Chicago." Acknowledging Galluzzo in 1995, when *Dreams* was first published, "would have been a bit like calling yourself a protégé of ACORN founder Wade Rathke today," writes Kurtz. [62]

Rey Lopez-Calderone, a former Gamaliel Foundation community organizer, gave an insider's perspective on Galluzzo's confrontational approach to organizing.

He told *Foundation Watch*, a publication of the Capital Research Institute, that "Galluzzo told me that he wanted organizers to be tough bastards who could build power like the Conquistadors."

Galluzzo had a seminar with a segment titled, "Walking the Edge of Immorality," in which trainees were taught to be "ruthless," Lopez-Calderone said. "It talked about how, if people are getting in the way of what you want to achieve as an organizer, you should be willing to push those people out of your way," he recalled. Galluzzo repeatedly stressed in the seminar that "the ends justify the means," said Lopez-Calderone. "The idea was to get people to make shady decisions in order to build power." [63]

The Community Organizing Socialist John McKnight, Mentor In Anti-Capitalist Organizing

John McKnight is a leftist academic, activist, and another of Barack Obama's neighborhood organizing mentors. A former Illinois director of the American Civil Liberties Union, he is co-founder of the Center for Urban Affairs Policy Research at Northwestern University, where he is now professor emeritus. McKnight has expertise in both community organizing and health policy. He has been a Gamaliel Foundation Board member and served, as did Dr. Jeremiah Wright and Father Michael Pfleger, on the advisory board of a youth counseling program launched by Obama in 1987.

McKnight also recommended Obama to Harvard Law School. Speaking to a small audience, McKnight recalled how Obama had said, "'You're the only professor I know,'" when asking for a letter of recommendation. McKnight added, jocularly, but also curiously, "I think he didn't do too well in college." [64]

McKnight co-authored a 1984 paper likely read by Obama that advocates a new strategy to lift organizer's sights above small-ball skirmishes with city hall or local businesses to actions targeted at restructuring the economy. Using the Community Reinvestment Act, which forces lending institutions to make "sub-prime loans" to high credit-risk customers, as a model, McKnight and his co-author John Kretzmann argued for burdening other industries with CRA-like requirements as a means to redistribute private wealth and, presumably, "achieve economic justice." By distorting housing lending decisions CRA had a role in the 2008 economic crisis. However, McKnight wants the same kind of law applied across the economy, with predictable and catastrophic consequences.

Author Stanley Kurtz, a close student of the Obama network, observes that:

> McKnight and Kretzmann want to impose CRA-like redistributive constraints on a whole range of industries. For example, they favor laws that would give community organizers a place on corporate boards and regulatory agencies, thereby preventing businesses from leaving a community at will. Just as ACORN inserted itself into America's banking system through CRA, McKnight and Kretzmann want organizers to press for laws that would give them influence over the entire system of production. This movement to place constraints on capitalism "from below" was the strategy favored by the Democratic Socialists of America (DSA) in the eighties. This socialist vision, I argue, inspired Obama to become a

community organizer. He learned how to go
about it from his mentor John McKnight. [65]

McKnight's socialist impulses are also displayed in his
health care policy work. The co-founder with Dr.
Quentin Young of the Health and Medicine Policy
Research Group, he has long championed a single-
payer health care system. *Health & Medicine*, a
magazine published by the Health and Medicine Policy
Research Group in the 1980s is "filled with socialist
themes," notes Kurtz.

The Winter 1985 issue speaks favorably about health
care under the Marxist Sandinistas in Nicaragua.
Also in that issue, Quentin Young interviews
McKnight on Sweden's welfare state, a topic on
which McKnight has expertise. McKnight notes that
Sweden's 52 percent tax rate (add to that its 15
percent national sales tax) probably maxes out the
taxpayer's capacity to pay. A solution favored by
leftists in Sweden to get even more out of taxpayers
is to tax the time of its citizens, requiring them to
provide manual labor in state institutions, a policy
that would also put an upper limit on the amount
of time a Swede could devote to working for his own
private profit.

Young and McKnight are not disturbed by a
proposal that amounts to slave labor. While they
"acknowledge the radicalism of this proposal,"
Kurtz writes, "they clearly admire the Swedish
system and are at least open to the idea of
compulsory citizen labor. Such are the values of
Obama's organizing mentors and political collaborators." [66]

7

Radical Unrepentant Terrorist

Bill Ayers, Obama's Political Partner

Obama likely first met unrepentant domestic terrorist Bill Ayers in 1988 when both were working on school reform in Chicago, a concern on which the two men also collaborated from 1995 to 2001 when they dished out more than $100 million as leaders of the Chicago Annenberg Challenge.

Kurtz reports that Bill Ayers' brother, John, met Obama as early as 1987. John Ayers was a leader in the Chicago school reform network that brother Bill joined upon his return to Chicago to begin teaching at the University of Illinois. Kurtz notes that Obama "was working with just about every leader in the movement for Chicago school reform months before Bill Ayers arrived on the scene" and that Ayers has written that his best friends in Chicago are his colleagues and co-workers from the late 1980s school-reform battles. Since, as Kurtz writes, "Obama was a member in good standing of that circle from the start," [67] how could the two men have not met and worked together from 1988 onward? And since Obama and Ayers later worked together on two foundations and teamed up to campaign against a juvenile crime reform bill, how could Obama, a

Harvard Law School graduate, not have known about Ayers' violent and revolutionary past? And, of course, Obama's political career was launched in the Ayers/Dohrn home. All of this suggests much more than a mere passing familiarity between the two men. Nonetheless, Obama wants us to believe that Bill Ayers is just a "guy who lives in my neighborhood...who I know."

Bill Ayers is a unrepentant former leader of the Weather Underground, a violent group that declared war on "Amerikkka" in 1969. An offshoot from Students for a Democratic Society, the Weather Underground claimed credit for some 25 bombings, including attacks on the U.S. Capitol, Pentagon and police stations in the early 1970s. DiscovertheNetworks.org reports that Ayers called the Weather Underground an "American Red Army" and said its mission statement was "Kill all the rich people. Break up their cars and apartments. Bring the revolution home. Kill your parents." [68]

In his 2001 memoir *Fugitive Days*, Ayers writes that "Everything was absolutely ideal on the day I bombed the Pentagon. The sky was blue. Birds were singing. And the bastards were finally going to get what was coming to them." [69]

A better title for Ayers' rehash of life as a '60s antiwar radical might be "No Regrets." Ayers seems to have none. He writes toward the end of his book, "Of all those fugitive days—of all those terrible and exquisite years—I regret nothing for myself." [70] Nor can he say he wouldn't do it again. "I can't quite imagine putting a bomb in a building today— all of that seems so distinctly a part of then. But I can't imagine entirely dismissing the possibility, either." [71] Ayers served with Barack Obama on the board of the Chicago Annenberg Challenge when he wrote this. Ayers' wife, Bernardine Dohrn, now an associate professor of law at Northwestern University, was also a Weather Underground leader. FBI informant Larry Grathwohl told a Senate subcommittee in 1974 that Ayers said in his hearing that Dohrn planned the bombing of a San Francisco police station and planted the bomb which killed 24-year-old San Francisco patrol officer Brian McDonnell on Feb. 16, 1970.

According to Grathwohl, Ayers on another occasion dismissed concern over the possible death of innocents from a planned bomb attack. "We can't protect all the innocent people in the world," Ayers reportedly said. "Some will get killed. Some of us will get killed. We have to accept that fact." [72]

Grathwohl recalls Weather Underground organizers discussing what would come after the revolution. They talked of re-education camps in the Southwest U.S. to reorient intransigent and liberty-loving Americans away from capitalism toward communism. Those who refused to go along with a new Marxist political order would be "eliminated."

In a 1982 documentary, *No Place to Hide*, Grathwohl shared his recollections:

> I [Grathwohl] asked, "Well what is going to happen to those people we can't reeducate, that are diehard capitalists?" And the reply was that they'd have to be eliminated.

> And when I pursued this further, they estimated they would have to eliminate 25 million people in these reeducation centers.

And when I say "eliminate," I mean "kill."

Twenty-five million people.

I want you to imagine sitting in a room with 25 people, most of which have graduate degrees from Columbia and other well-known educational centers, and hear them figuring out the logistics for the elimination of 25 million people.

And they were dead serious. [73]

Dohrn shared in the revolutionary bloodlust. She celebrated the Manson Family murders in which movie star, Sharon Tate, then nine months pregnant, and seven others were mercilessly stabbed and killed. The words "Death to Pigs" were smeared with the victims' blood on a wall. Speaking at a 1969 Weather Underground War Council, Dohrn exclaimed:

Dig it! First they killed those pigs and then they put a fork in pig Tate's belly. Wild!... Offing those rich pigs with their own forks and knives, and then eating a meal in the same room, far out! The Weathermen dig Charles Manson! [74]

The revolutionary ardor of Ayers and Dohrn is blatant in their saber-rattling 1974 book, *Prairie Fire: The Politics of Revolutionary Anti-Imperialism*, which has the following statements:

- "We are a guerrilla organization. We are communist women and men ... deeply affected by the historic events of our time in the struggle against U.S. imperialism."

- "Our intention is to disrupt the empire, to

incapacitate it, to put pressure on the cracks, to make it hard to carry out its bloody functioning against the people of the world, to join the world struggle, to attack from the inside."

- "The only path to the final defeat of imperialism and the building of socialism is revolutionary war."

- "Revolutionary war will be complicated and protracted. It includes mass struggle and clandestine struggle, peaceful and violent, political and economic, cultural and military, where all forms are developed in harmony with the armed struggle."

- "Without mass struggle there can be no revolution. Without armed struggle there can be no victory."

- "We need a revolutionary communist party in order to lead the struggle, give coherence and direction to the fight, seize power and build the new society."

- "Our job is to tap the discontent seething in many sectors of the population, to find allies everywhere people are hungry or angry, to mobilize poor and working people against imperialism."

- "Socialism is the total opposite of capitalism/imperialism. It is the rejection of empire and white supremacy. Socialism is the violent overthrow of the bourgeoisie, the establishment of the dictatorship of the proletariat, and the eradication of the social system based on profit." [75]

Ayers and Dohrn spent the 1970s underground and escaped prison for their crimes on a technicality. They are no longer planting bombs, but they show no contrition for their past deeds. When the couple surfaced and gave themselves up to authorities on December 3, 1980, they held a press conference at which Dohrn showed her revolutionary flame burned as hot as ever. "Resistance by every means necessary is happening and will continue to happen within the United States as well as around the world," she said, "and I remain committed to the struggle ahead." [76]

For his part, Ayers said in 2001, "I don't regret setting bombs. I feel we didn't do enough." [77]

It turns out that in the years since the bombs went off, Ayers has done a great deal more, working from within the system to overthrow capitalism, a goal to which he remains committed. To reach his goal, Ayers has turned to education reform and community organizing, two enterprises lavishly funded by his friend and partner Barack Obama.

8

From Annenberg
To Woods

How Obama and Ayers
Funded The Revolution

Bill Ayers has been in hot pursuit of "education reform" ever since his return to Chicago in 1987. He revealed what he hopes to achieve by revamping American education in 2006 when he sat beside Venezuelan dictator Hugo Chavez at an education forum in Caracas, and declared his support for...

> ...the profound educational reforms under way here in Venezuela under the leadership of President Chávez. *We share the belief that education is the motor-force of revolution....* I look forward to seeing how you continue to overcome the failings of capitalist education as you seek to create something truly new and deeply humane. [78]

Revolution, it seems clear, is what motivated Bill Ayers to found the Chicago Annenberg Challenge, a five-year school reform effort bankrolled by billionaire Walter Annenberg. Ayers was the CAC's "guiding spirit," Kurtz writes, and one of five individuals who led the CAC during its first year after which Barack Obama was chosen as chairman. With more than

$100 million to give away, Ayers had a clear interest in who became chairman, making Obama's appointment telling evidence of Ayers' confidence in Obama's ideological reliability. Even friendly biographer David Remnick reports that "Ayers helped bring Obama onto the Annenberg board." [79]

A look at who got funded and the types of projects to which the CAC gave away its millions shows Ayers' confidence was well placed. Board minutes reviewed by Kurtz reveal, he writes, that "Mr. Obama and Mr. Ayers worked as a team to advance the CAC agenda"—which is to say Mr. Ayers' agenda.

DiscovertheNetworks.org reports that:

> Under Ayers' stewardship, CAC scarcely focused at all on measures aimed at improving student performance in traditional curricular studies, but rather was guided by Ayers' belief – as outlined in his book *Teaching Toward Freedom* – that the primary duty of educators was to "teach against [the] oppression" that allegedly pervaded American society, and to thereby encourage revolution and social transformation. [80]

One especially curious feature of CAC was its decision not to fund schools directly, but to hand out money to "external partners." The CAC, under Obama's leadership, turned down groups that help students do better in math and science while writing checks for radical organizations—ones friendly to both Obama and Ayers, including the Association of Community Organizations for Reform Now (ACORN); Obama's former group, Developing Communities Project; and the Small Schools Workshop, an Ayers project which received $1,056,162 from the CAC. [81]

The result of showering millions on radical outside groups was a very expensive failure. More than $100 million was spent without even an uptick in how students from low-performing schools do on tests. That is the conclusion of the CAC's own internal report. [82] Barack Obama spent five years doling out millions of dollars and wound up with almost nothing to show for it. It was an expensive dress rehearsal for his later attempt, also failed, to goose the American economy by flooding it with billions of tax dollars. Both failures have been met with listless disinterest from most in the media.

Kurtz lays the blame for CAC's failure not on the intractability of education improvement, but "the shared desire of Obama and Ayers to funnel a very large pot of money to the city's most radical community organizers." It was, he writes, a case of "leftist political patronage, pure and simple. Ayers chose Obama for the job because he knew Obama could be trusted to support Chicago's socialist network. After all, Obama was already doing the very same thing at the Woods Fund." [83]

Not only was Obama well-positioned to fund his friends, allies, and political partners on the left as chairman of the Chicago Annenberg Challenge, he did the same for a decade as a board member and later vice chairman and chairman of the Woods Fund. Obama joined the Woods Fund board in 1994, a year after the Fund split in two after a long tussle between a group of board members interested in funding the arts and a radical faction focused on community organizing. The split left the radicals with 70 percent of the Woods endowment and the flow of dollars to community organizing picked up in 1994 after Obama joined the board and reviewed

Woods fund support for organizing groups.

With Obama on board, the Woods Fund gave money in 1996 to Bernardine Dohrn's Children and Family Justice Center at Northwestern University School of Law. And in 1999, Ayers joined Obama on the board, which led, Kurtz reports, to even more money going to community organizing groups. Among the organizations that got in on the gravy train were ACORN, the Midwest Academy, and far-left advocates on juvenile justice issues, [84] a cause on which Ayers and Obama co-labored in the late 1990s when they joined forces to fight a juvenile justice reform measure in the Illinois legislature.

The more one knows about the boards and causes shared by Obama and Ayers, the less one can entertain, much less believe, candidate Obama's 2008 claim that Ayers is just a "guy who lives in my neighborhood...who I know."

Mutual friend and long-time leftist activist Quentin Young calls them "friends," but their long history of work together makes them more than that. They are political partners.

And literary collaborators as well, according to Christopher Andersen, author of the 2009 book, *Barack and Michelle: Portrait of a Marriage*. He writes that Obama, at Michelle's urging, enlisted Ayers in early 1994 to help finish the manuscript for *Dreams from My Father*, a lagging project due that September. Obama delivered taped oral histories from his Kenyan relatives, "along with a partial manuscript and a truckload of notes," to Ayers, a veteran writer. "In the end," Andersen writes, "Ayers' contribution to Barack's *Dreams from My Father* would be significant— so much so that the book's language, oddly specific references, literary devices, and themes would bear a jarring similarity to Ayers' own writing." [85]

One more signal of the Ayers-Obama link is Obama's 1995 political debut, which took place at the home of Dohrn and Ayers in Hyde Park. It was here that Illinois state senator and starry-eyed Soviet sympathizer Alice Palmer informed the gathering that Barack was her anointed successor.

Team Obama

9

The Communist-Loving Predecessor

Alice Palmer, Soviet Dupe
Who Hand-Picked Obama

C hicago's Hyde Park neighborhood is one of America's most progressive enclaves. It's been called "Berkeley with snow." So when Alice Palmer decided to resign her Illinois Senate seat representing Hyde Park and environs to run for Congress, she picked a man who was a known entity and whose ideology closely mirrored her own—someone who would satisfy her far-left Hyde Park constituents. And she gathered a likeminded group in the home of Bill Ayers and Bernardine Dohrn to make her announcement.

"I can remember being one of a small group of people who came to Bill Ayers' house to learn that Alice Palmer was stepping down from the Senate and running for Congress," Dr. Quentin Young, a socialist activist and well-known Chicago physician told Politico. "[Palmer] identified [Obama] as her successor." [86]

Kurtz believes Palmer picked Obama after consulting with others in her socialist-friendly network, some of whom were linked to the Midwest Academy, a neighborhood organizing training outfit set up, Key Wiki reports, by "former members of the Students for a Democratic Society (SDS), the far-left activist group." The Academy's president is Heather Booth, the wife of a former SDS leader, Paul Booth. [87]

"Palmer and her Midwest Academy circle were savvy and tactically ruthless socialist ideologues," observes Kurtz. "It's tough to imagine them surrendering Hyde Park's State Senate seat to someone who was not 'one of them.'" [88]

To get a better sense of who Obama is, it's worth taking a close look at Alice Palmer.

An educator and activist who served in the Illinois Senate from 1991 to 1997, Palmer has a long history of familiarity and friendship with socialist and communist causes. The government of Grenada sent her an official invitation in 1980 to come celebrate the Caribbean nation's Cuban/Soviet-backed revolution. She served from 1983-85 on the board of the U.S. Peace Council, which was heavily influenced by the Communist Party USA and campaigned for nuclear disarmament.

Palmer attended the World Peace Council's convention in Prague in 1983, the year in which the Soviet campaign for a nuclear freeze commenced. She traveled in 1985 with other black journalists to East bloc nations, including the Soviet Union, East Germany, and Czechoslovakia. Palmer was in Moscow in 1986 to cover the 27th Congress of the Communist Party of the Soviet Union as a writer for the *Black Press Institute*, which she and her husband established in the early 1980s. *New Deliberations,* a *Black Press Institute* journal, published articles such as "Socialism is the Only Way Forward" and

"Is Black Bourgeoise Ideology Enough?" [89]

Palmer was dazzled and deluded by what she saw and experienced in Moscow at the party congress. She told the *People's Daily World,* the official newspaper of the Communist Party USA, that:

> I spent a great deal of time with a woman from the Novosti (Press Agency) and she and I had a lot in common...I had a chance to go shopping, just as I would if were back in Chicago...It is useful to those people who would like to demonize the Soviet people. When I stood in line, it was the same kind of line I stand in in the Jewel grocery store in Chicago. It was merely because the place was crowded, not because at the end of the line there was nothing for me to purchase. [90]

In a report on the party congress published in the *People's Daily World,* Palmer spoke favorably about "central planning" and gave readers a pro-Soviet perspective:

> We Americans can be misled by the major media. We're being told the Soviets are striving to achieve a comparatively low standard of living compared with ours, but actually they have reached a basic stability in meeting their needs and are now planning to double their production. [91]

Palmer, according to DiscovertheNetworks.org, "marveled that all Russian citizens were guaranteed employment to match their training and skills, as well as free education, affordable housing, and free medical care." [92]

Given her socialist sensibilities, Palmer found in Obama a man with whom she had several meetings prior to her Hyde Park announcement, someone to carry the torch for progressive politics into the Illinois Senate. As Kurtz writes, "Obama was chosen to succeed Alice Palmer in the Illinois State Senate because, like Palmer and her close political circle, Obama was a socialist." [93]

That charge is reinforced by the endorsement Obama earned from the socialist New Party in his run for state senate. And by the fact that he not only earned an endorsement, he also joined the party.

10

A Confirmed Socialist

Obama's "New Party" Membership

F ounded in 1992 by members of the Democratic Socialists of America, ACORN, and the SEIU (Service Employees International Union), the New Party's aim was to move the Democratic Party to the extreme left. Its founding members included linguist Noam Chomsky; Marxist intellectuals Manning Marable and Cornel West; Frances Fox Piven, co-author of the "Cloward-Piven strategy;" former SDS leader Todd Gitlin; historian Howard Zinn; Gloria Steinem; and Barbara Ehrenreich.

As might be expected from a political body launched by socialists and friends, the New Party, "believes that the social, economic, and political progress of the United States requires a democratic revolution in America— the return of power to the people." [94]

What that revolution entails is spelled out in the New Party's statement of principles which calls for a 'sustainable economy," shorter work week, guaranteed wages, universal health care and child care, lifelong access to education, defense cuts, progressive taxation, and absolute abortion rights. The New Party also wants to socialize the American economy by ending private ownership and replacing it with "popular election of those charged with public stewardship of our banking system, worker-owner control over their pension assets, community-controlled alternative financial institutions." [95]

It all sounds socialist but in keeping with the Left's use of stealth to cloak ultimate political aims, the New Party did not wear the socialist label. Still, New Party co-founders Daniel Cantor and Joel Rogers wrote in a strategy memo, cited by Kurtz, that they wanted the New Party to be "an explicitly social democratic organization, with an ideology roughly like that of Northern European (e.g., Swedish) labor movements." [96] Which is to say the New Party was socialist.

Intrepid investigative blogger Trevor Loudon unearthed strong indication in 2008 of Obama's New Party membership, locating a Spring 1996 *New Party News* report stating that "New Party members won three other primaries this Spring in Chicago: Barack Obama (State Senate), Michael Chandler (Democratic Party Committee) and Patricia Martin (Cook County Judiciary)...." [97]

Other documentation indicating Obama's New Party membership include a New Party primary election results announcement listing Obama as a member,[98] and a reference to Obama as a New Party member in the *Progressive Populist*. [99]

Despite the evidence, the Obama campaign vehemently denied in 2008 that Obama held membership in the de facto socialist New Party. Fight the Smears, an Obama campaign website, blasted "Right-wing hatchet man and conspiracy theorist, Stanley Kurtz" for his "crackpot smear against Barack falsely claiming he was a member of something called the New Party:" [100]

While existing evidence weighed heavily in favor of

Obama's New Party membership, the question remained unresolved until June 2012 when Kurtz unearthed minutes from the January 11, 1996, meeting of the New Party's Chicago chapter, which read as follows:

> Barack Obama, candidate for State Senate in the 13th Legislative District, gave a statement to the membership and answered questions. He signed the New Party "Candidate Contract" and requested an endorsement from the New Party. He also joined the New Party. [101]

Kurtz also cited a membership list of New Party Chicago members which shows Obama as a member who joined on January 11, 1996. The Obama campaign is unfazed by the evidence. Despite documentation from actual New Party minutes, the campaign still denies Obama's New Party membership. Denial may be Obama's only "good" option. To acknowledge Obama's membership in a far-left political party with a socialist program would open his Chicago socialist connections to scrutiny and prove hazardous to his political prospects, perhaps fatal.

That's why he cannot afford to acknowledge the truth. The same goes for his long-standing relationship to ACORN, the Association of Community Organizations for Reform Now.

Team Obama

11
ACORN

Obama's "Old Friend"
And Organizing Cohort

I n their final presidential debate on October 15, 2008, GOP challenger John McCain brought up Obama's ACORN connection and said the nation ought to know "the full extent of Sen. Obama's relationship with ACORN."

"The only involvement I've had with ACORN," Obama shot back, "was I represented them alongside the U.S. Justice Department in making Illinois implement a Motor Voter Law." [102]

His campaign took an even harder line, lashing out at "naked lies about his supposed connection to ACORN" and claimed that "ACORN was not part of Project VOTE!, the successful voter registration drive Barack ran in 1992." [103]

Barack told ACORN leaders something else entirely in 2007 when seeking ACORN's endorsement for his presidential bid. In a video that came to light after the 2008 election, Obama is shown touting his long and close ties to ACORN "my entire career," from Project VOTE! to his service in the U.S. Senate:

> When I ran Project VOTE!, voter registration drive in Illinois, ACORN was smack dab in

the middle of it. Once I was elected, there wasn't a campaign that ACORN worked on down in Springfield that I wasn't right there with you. Since I've been in the United States Senate, I've always been a partner with ACORN as well. I've been fighting with ACORN, alongside ACORN, on issues you care about, my entire career. [104]

ACORN, or the Association of Community Organizations for Reform Now, is a radical group founded in 1970 by former SDS member Wade Rathke. As of 2008, ACORN had more than 400,000 dues-paying members and 1,200-plus chapters in 110 U.S. cities. It has been implicated in voter-registration fraud cases, as well as vote-rigging and voter intimidation cases, according to DiscovertheNetworks.org.[105] It has taken in $126.4 million in donations and tax dollars since 1993.[106] It also took aim in the 1980s and 1990s at the U.S. banking system, using confrontational tactics and the Community Reinvestment Act to help "drag America's banking system into the business of subprime lending,"[107] a leading factor in America's 2008 financial crisis. Throughout the 80s and 90s, Kurtz writes, "Obama did everything in his power to support ACORN's work." [108]

ACORN came to the attention of most Americans in 2009 when secretly recorded video showed ACORN officials at numerous locations offering to assist a pimp and prostitute in their effort to run a prostitution ring using minor girls from Central America. The fallout from that debacle forced ACORN to reorganize, disbanding itself as a national entity but still pursuing its radical mission via state groups using different names.

Staged confrontations in pursuit of far-left goals are

a large part of the ACORN modus operandi. The Capital Research Center offers this review of the range of concerns that animate ACORN:

> ACORN ... organizes crude protests against businesspeople and public officials. Opposed to the profit motive and capitalism in general, it pushes for more government control over citizens and the economy. ACORN supports gun control, a government monopoly in healthcare and an open door immigration policy. It supports a big raise in the federal minimum wage and so-called 'living-wage' laws enacted by states and cities. ACORN wants more funding for urban public schools, and wants federal and state laws enacted guaranteeing paid sick leave for all full-time workers. The group claims to fight for affordable housing and it rails against foreclosures and so-called 'predatory' lending, even though it demands that banks make loans [to under-qualified borrowers] destined to default. [109]

While ACORN does not label itself a socialist organization, others on the far left recognize that it serves the socialist cause. The newsletter of the DSOC (Democratic Socialist Organizing Committee) declared that "Democratic socialists must participate in and support [ACORN's] efforts, not as ideological outsiders with a separate agenda, but as committed allies in the same struggle." [110]

Kurtz notes that the other major socialist organization in the U.S. in the 1970s, the New American Movement, reached the same conclusion about ACORN and its ideology:

> ACORN is an integral part of the evolving
> forces of socialism, *even if not consciously so*
> [emphasis original] ... it is an organization of
> people's power in the communities, and is thus
> central to the institutional framework of a
> future democratic socialism....[111]

In 1992, Obama ran Project VOTE!, a voter registration initiative which helped Carol Mosely Braun win election to the U.S. Senate. The Obama campaign has denied ACORN's involvement in Project VOTE!, but Project VOTE!'s Steering Committee included both Madeline Talbott, the head of Chicago ACORN, and Keith Kelleher, chief organizer of the ACORN-controlled SEIU Local 880. According to Kelleher:

> Local 880 and Illinois ACORN joined forces
> with a newly invigorated voter registration
> group, Project VOTE!, run by former
> community organizer (and current Democratic
> presidential candidate and U.S. Senator)
> Barack Obama, to bring other community
> groups under the Project VOTE! umbrella and
> move a large-scale voter registration program
> for U.S. Senator Carol Moseley Braun.[112]

Obama also helped train ACORN leaders starting in 1992, winning praise from Chicago ACORN chief Madeline Talbott, who said, "Barack has proven himself among our members. He is committed to organizing, to building a democracy. Above all else, he is a good listener, and we accept and respect him as a kindred spirit, a fellow organizer." [113]

The respect and admiration was mutual. Obama served on the boards of two organizations, the Woods Fund and the Chicago Annenberg Challenge (CAC) that funneled significant dollars into

ACORN coffers. Both Obama and Chicago ACORN head Talbott served together in 1994 on the Woods Fund community-organizing advisory board, and saw Woods funding for ACORN jump that year.[114] The Woods Fund gave at least five grants to ACORN during Obama's tenure on the board: $ 45,000 (2000), $ 30,000 (2001), $45,000 (2001), $ 30,000 (2002), and $ 40,000 (2002).[115] The CAC gave more than $400,000 between 1997 and 2002 to the Grassroots School Improvement Campaign, a joint project of Chicago ACORN, Bill Ayers' Small Schools Workshop, Cross City Campaign for Urban School Reform, and eight Chicago schools.[116]

The tight friendship between Obama and ACORN displayed in the largesse he helped deliver to the community organizing group and the training he did for ACORN, helped motivate ACORN workers to serve on his political campaigns. Toni Foulkes, a Chicago ACORN leader and a member of ACORN's National Association Board, wrote about the work ACORN did to get out the vote for Obama in his successful 2004 Senate primary campaign. That election, Foulkes wrote, was an occasion on which the supposedly non-partisan group could "have our cake and eat it too: work on nonpartisan voter registration and GOTV, which also turns out to benefit the candidate that we hold dear."

Foulkes writes that ACORN first noticed Obama "when he was organizing on the far south side of the city with the Developing Communities Project," adding, "He was a very good organizer." After law school, the relationship grew, Foulkes writes, as "we [ACORN] asked him to help us with a [motor voter] lawsuit." Next came Obama's work in 1992 for the

ACORN-influenced Project VOTE!. The relationship continued to grow after that and Obama reaped a political dividend, as Foulkes detailed:

> Since then we have invited Obama to our leadership training sessions to run the session on power every year, and, as a result, many of our newly developing leaders got to know him before he ever ran for office. Thus, it was natural for many of us to be active volunteers in his first campaign for State Senate and then his failed bid for U.S. Congress in 1996 [sic]. By the time he ran for U.S. Senate, we were old friends.[117]

Another old friend is the Rev. Dr. Jeremiah Wright, Obama's long-time pastor, mentor and spiritual advisor.

12

The Wright Stuff For Radical Theology

Jeremiah Wright, Obama's Black Liberation Pastor

B arack Obama met Jeremiah Wright in the late 1980s when the young community organizer was enlisting black churches into his Developing Communities Project. Wright warned Obama then that the involvement of his church, Trinity United Church of Christ, could be a liability to his cause.

"I'll try to help you if I can," he said. "But you should know that having us involved in your effort isn't necessarily a feather in your cap." "Why's that?" Reverend Wright shrugged. "Some of my fellow clergy don't appreciate what we're about. They feel like we're too radical. Others, we ain't radical enough." 118

Given what is now known about Wright and his church, it's hard to imagine anyone complaining that Wright's church was not radical *enough*. Wright was certainly radical enough for two local religious extremists, Father Michael Pfleger and Minister Louis Farrakhan, both of whom Wright counts as friends.

Despite Wright's caution, Obama was not dissuaded and, in time, joined Trinity, forming a 20-year relationship with Wright, a disciple of Black Liberation theologian James Cone, and frequent flyer to Cuba, which he visited twice in the mid-1980s. Obama married Michelle at Trinity in a ceremony officiated by Wright who later baptized their two daughters. The family routinely attended Trinity, "every week, eleven o'clock service," as Obama told an interviewer in 2004. [119]

Obama's Wright problem first erupted in February 2007, the month Obama announced his candidacy, when *Rolling Stone* profiled "Rev. Jeremiah Wright, a sprawling, profane bear of a preacher." The article rehearsed a sermon in which Wright ticked off ten "facts" about America, one of which was that "Racism is how this country was founded and how this country is still run!" a claim met with "thumping applause." Amid "whoops and amens" from the crowd, Wright reached his sonorous climax: "And. And. And! GOD! Has GOT! To be SICK! OF THIS SHIT!" [120]

The article had limited impact on Obama's campaign, but a year later it all hit the fan when video of Wright's angry pulpit rants went viral. One clip showed Wright blasting America on the Sunday after 9/11 when 19 Muslim terrorists had killed nearly 3,000 Americans:

> We bombed Hiroshima, we bombed Nagasaki, and we nuked far more than the thousands in New York and the Pentagon, and we never batted an eye... and now we are indignant, because the stuff we have done overseas is now brought back into our own front yards. America's chickens are coming home to roost.[121]

Along with the rest of the nation, Obama said he

was shocked by what he heard. After disagreeing with Wright's comments but professing allegiance to the man, Obama ultimately distanced himself from Wright and left Trinity.

But until Wright became a political liability to Obama's path to the White House, Obama had been happy to have the pastor of the 8,000 member Trinity United Church of Christ be called his mentor and friend. "What I value most about Pastor Wright," Obama said in happier times, "is not his day-to-day political advice. He's much more of a sounding board for me to make sure that I am speaking as truthfully about what I believe as possible and that I'm not losing myself in some of the hype and hoopla and stress that's involved in national politics." [122]

Despite their tight bond over 20 years, Wright's caustic, hate-filled diatribes, which gave most Americans their first introduction to Black Liberation Theology, somehow went unnoticed by Obama. Statements like "Jesus was a black man" and "God damn America" were never spoken in Obama's hearing until, along with the rest of the nation, he learned about Wright's radical bent in 2008.

Right.

What Obama heard as he attended Trinity week by week was what fellow congregant Oprah Winfrey also heard. Wright's inflammatory and angry pulpiteering was a major reason she left the church by the mid-1990s.[123] Not Obama. He must have been gone those Sundays. "Most of the time, when I'm in church," Obama said innocently, "he's talking about Jesus, God, faith, values, caring for the poor...." [124]

That, and other denials of his knowledge of Wright,

"was deeply dishonest," says researcher Stanley Kurtz. He notes that the two men had an intellectual bond. As Wright told an Obama biographer, "We talked about race and politics." Obama was familiar with the incendiary views of Wright's intellectual mentor, Black Liberation theologian James Cone, and intentionally chose Wright's church, Trinity United Church of Christ "in full knowledge of Wright's radical theological views..." and "precisely *because* of those radical views." [125]

It's no surprise Obama acted as he did to distance himself from Wright and deny any knowledge of his pastor's radical beliefs. He had to. Like ACORN, like Ayers, like his New Party membership, like his work on the boards of the Woods Fund and the Chicago Annenberg Challenge, Wright is one more window into Obama's socialist past, something Obama had to hide at all costs in 2008 from the American public in order to make it into the Oval Office.

Wright is a follower of theologian James Cone, author in 1969 of *Black Theology and Black Power,* and a professor at Union Theological Seminary. Cone's Black Liberation Theology is a deeply racist, anti-white, angry, and grotesquely distorted take on Christianity. Cone regards the U.S. as a "racist society"[126] and demonizes whites, writing that "whiteness is the symbol of the antichrist." He applauds "Malcolm X [who] was not far wrong when he called the white man 'the devil.'" [127]

The solution, for Cone, "is the destruction of whiteness, which is the source of human misery in the world." [128] White oppression obligates the black intellectual, Cone says, to "aid in the destruction of America as he knows it." [129] Giving fresh meaning to the term "tough love," Cone wrote in 1970 that

"What we need is the divine love as expressed in Black Power, which is the power of Black people to destroy their oppressors here and now by any means at their disposal." [130]

Cone addressed the 1984 Socialist Scholars Conference, which Obama likely attended, and visited Cuba that same year with Wright and others. Cone links capitalism to racism, which is why both must be eliminated. "Perhaps what we need today," wrote Cone, "is to return to that 'good old-time religion' of our grandparents and combine it with a Marxist critique of society. Together black religion and Marxist philosophy may show us the way to build a completely new society." [131]

Cone's radical views were hailed and followed at Wright's Trinity United Church of Christ. So much so that Cone told a reporter that Trinity most fully embodies his message. [132] Cone praised Wright as "really the one who took it from my books and brought it to the church." [133] He called Wright " a perfect example and expression of Black Liberation Theology." [134] As Kurtz writes, "Obama arguably belonged to the most radical black church in the country." [135]

Like his mentor Cone, Wright is a friend to Marxism who fulminates against America, white racism, and capitalism. Wright traveled to Cuba twice, and told his flock about his enduring links there in a 2006 sermon:

> I have been affiliated with the Cuba Council of Churches since the 1980s. I have several close Cuban friends who work with the Cuba Council of Churches and you have heard me preach about our affiliation and the Black

Theology Project's trips to Cuba. The Cuban Council of Churches has been a non-partisan global mission partner for decades. I have worked with them for two decades. [136]

Far from non-partisan, the Cuban Council of Churches, as author Humberto Fontova observes, is controlled by Cuba's secret police, the DGI.[137]

Wright's leftist politics were on display again in 2009 when he helped the socialist magazine *Monthly Review* celebrate its 60th anniversary, praising it for its "no-nonsense Marxism" and insulting America as the "land of the greed and home of the slave." [138] As a minister, he let it pass that Marxism is atheistic and brought mass murder to millions.

Wright has incorporated Black Liberation Theology into the ministry vision of Trinity United Church of Christ. Its "10-point vision" bristles with Wright's anti-capitalist perspective. Among the points is the cultivation of "a congregation working towards ECONOMIC PARITY" (emphasis in original.) And the church mission statement sets out the goal of helping "the less fortunate to become agents of change for God who is not pleased with America's economic mal-distribution!" [139]

All this and more could not have escaped Obama's attention. In *Dreams from My Father*, Obama quotes Wright saying in his "Audacity of Hope" sermon that, "White folks' greed runs a world in need." Similar "harshly spoken anti-capitalist tirades are so pervasive in Wright's sermons and publications," Kurtz writes, "that Obama had to have seen them." 140

For example, new member classes at Trinity include

instruction in black liberation theology which is also contained in literature packets given to new members, as the Obama campaign confirmed in 2007. "Both Obama and his wife have attended these classes," *Investor's Business Daily* pointed out, "so it stands to reason they have been indoctrinated into the radical theology." [141]

Obama's first exposure to Cone came in the 1980s. John Kretzmann, an Obama mentor and associate of John McKnight, told author Sasha Abramsky that Obama read Cone while working as a community organizer in Chicago.[142]

Cone finds Obama's public views consistent with his own. "I don't see anything in (Obama's) books or in the (Philadelphia race) speech that contradicts Black Liberation Theology," Cone said in 2008. In another interview, Cone said Obama's message "doesn't have as much of a radical edge to it.... He couldn't succeed with my message." [143]

Give Cone credit for a keen grasp of the obvious. His message hardly resonates within the black community, let alone the public at large. But one priest who has made it work is Father Michael Pfleger.

13

Barack's Leftist Priest

Father Pfleger, "Dear Friend" and Racial Divider

B arack Obama has known Rev. Michael Pfleger since at least 1987 when he recruited the radical Catholic priest to serve on the advisory committee of his youth counseling network, along with Rev. Jeremiah Wright. Pfleger's political partnership with Obama continued in 1992 when he joined other Obama allies from ACORN and SEIU on the Project VOTE! steering committee, a voter-registration effort that helped elect Carol Moseley Braun to the U.S. Senate.[144]

Pfleger, the long-time pastor of St. Sabina Catholic Church on Chicago's South Side, also chipped in financially to help Obama's state senate campaigns, giving $1,500 between 1995 and 2001. State Sen. Obama proved helpful in 2001 to Pfleger as well, steering state grants worth $225,000 to programs run by St. Sabina's.[145]

Obama told journalist Cathleen Falsani in 2004 that his "biggest challenge ... is always maintaining your moral compass," and said he counted Pfleger among the friends and advisers who help him keep his moral bearings.[146]

"Father Michael Pfleger is a dear friend," Obama

said, "and somebody I interact with closely."[147] So close that the two talked over Obama's aspiration to run for president.

"When Barack was thinking of running for president," Pfleger told Edward Klein, author of *The Amateur*, "I said to him: 'If you really believe that God is calling you to do this, forget all the norms. But don't forget that the only way this can happen is through God. If you believe God is calling you, do it. But don't forget, if you get it, don't forget it was God first, not people, who got you there.' And Barack said to me, 'Yes, Father, I really believe that my plan in life is to go and become president, and that God has called me to go now.'"[148]

Whether that conversation took place exactly as Pfleger recounts it is open to question, but the oratorically gifted leftist priest did give Obama his unqualified endorsement for president. He called Obama "the best thing to come across the political scene since Bobby Kennedy"[149] and served on the Catholics for Obama Committee, a group which advised the Obama campaign.[150]

He won't play that role this time around.

Like Wright, Pfleger had his own viral moment during the campaign after he stepped into the pulpit of Trinity United Church of Christ on May 25, 2008, to unleash a jeremiad against "white entitlement and supremacy," replete with a mean-spirited mockery of Hillary Clinton's tears. The crowd at Obama's home church laughed, cheered, and rose to their feet in approval. Unbeknown to Pfleger, it was all caught on video and live-streamed onto the Internet.

Nearly every TV news network in the nation quickly picked up on Pfleger's stinging performance. Obama immediately announced he was "deeply disappointed in Father Pfleger's divisive, backward-looking rhetoric" [151] and Pfleger's endorsement disappeared from Obama's campaign website.

The man Obama called "a dear friend, and somebody I interact with closely" had somehow, as with Wright, surprised and shocked Obama.

Pfleger, like Wright, is a severe critic of the U.S. who believes, as he said in his 2008 sermon at Trinity United, that "Racism is still America's greatest addiction" [152] and "America is the greatest sin against God." [153]

After the shooting death of Trayvon Martin, Pfleger, like many on the left, assumed that race was at the root of the tragic event. "We cannot talk about Trayvon Martin without talking about the racism that is alive and well in America today," he said. "America, we demand you deal with race." [154]

St. Sabina's, where Pfleger has pastored since 1981, has an enormous mural in its sanctuary depicting a black Jesus standing within the hands of God. It's an arresting signal of the influence of black liberation theologian James Cone on Pfleger who calls Roman Catholic leaders who fail to support Black Liberation Theology "pathetic and cowardly." Robert McClory, author of the Pfleger biography, *Radical Disciple*, remarks that "Black Liberation Theology is alive and well at St. Sabina." [155]

The dominant mural of a black Jesus inside the St. Sabina sanctuary fits well with Cone's startling claim that Jesus Christ is a black man. "Evidence exists within and outside the Bible to support the notion that the people of Israel, and the people of most of the empires and kingdoms that surrounded them at that time were of African descent." Cone enlists Rev. 1:14-15 to prove that Christ had "nappy hair" and "bronze skin." [156]

Pfleger says his views on race were formed by interaction with Black Panthers in the 1960s. "I got very educated by the [Black] Panthers — very educated," Pfleger told *Trumpet* magazine, which is published by Trinity United Church of Christ. [157]

> Pfleger thinks the government should pay reparations to black Americans for slavery, a position he touted in his May 2008 self-immolation at Trinity United. In one of his more memorable rhetorical riffs, Pfleger intoned:

Honestly now, to address the one who says, "Don't hold me responsible for what my ancestors did." But you have enjoyed the benefits of what your ancestors did ... and unless you are ready to give up the benefits, throw away your 401 fund, throw away your trust fund, throw away all the monies you put away into the company you walked into because your daddy and grand daddy ... Unless you are willing to give up the benefits then you must be responsible for what was done in your generation, because you are the beneficiaries of this insurance policy.[158]

Pfleger, like Wright, is a friend and apologist for Louis Farrakhan, the famously bow-tied anti-Semitic and anti-white leader of the Nation of Islam. "I have never found him to be anti-Semitic or anti-white," Father Pfleger told the *New York Times* in 1994. "I don't think there is any group or religion in America that has done more for the African-American male than the Nation of Islam. I feel the real problem is, America doesn't know how to handle Louis Farrakhan or the truth." [159]

The "truth," according to Farrakhan is that, "White people are *potential* humans ... they haven't evolved yet." Farrakhan has also denounced whites as "vicious beasts" and "the skunks of the planet." [160]

Pfleger and Farrakhan have visited in each other's home and Pfleger has hosted Farrakhan at his church on several occasions including in May 2008 when Farrakhan made an appearance after it was announced he was suffering from prostate cancer.

As Pfleger tells it, he is very closely linked to Farrakhan:

> "I've known the minister [Farrakhan] both as someone who I have great respect for as a prophetic voice, as a mentor but also as a friend and as a brother," said Pfleger. "We've become very close friends over the years. Our families have been close; he's shared dinner at my house as I have at his many, many times. He has preached from our pulpit here at this church on three different occasions. We've worked together on issues not only for this community but in the city and in the nation." [161]

Farrakhan is also tied to Pfleger's erstwhile "dear friend," Barack Obama. While our president distanced himself from Farrakhan as he ran for the presidency, he has been associated with his contro-versial Hyde Park neighbor in the past. So who is Louis Farrakhan and what are those links?

Team Obama

14

Making Obama
The Messiah

Louis Farrakhan, Radical Islamist
and Chicago Power Broker

Best known for calling Judaism a "gutter religion," [162] and lauding Hitler as a "very great man," [163] Nation of Islam leader Louis Farrakhan endorsed Obama for president in 2008, telling some 20,000 Nation of Islam followers that Illinois' junior senator was a herald of the Messiah, maybe the Messiah himself:

> Brothers and sisters, Barack Obama to me, is a herald of the Messiah. Barack Obama is like the trumpet that alerts you something new, something better is on the way.
>
> Young people, you are the instruments that God is gonna use to bring about universal change, and that is why Barack has captured the youth. And he has involved young people in a political process that they didn't care anything about. When the Messiah speaks, the young people will hear, and the Messiah is absolutely speaking. [164]

Farrakhan, who has a long history of angry, anti-Semitic, anti-white, and anti-American statements, enjoys warm relationships with Obama's one-time "dear friend" Michael Pfleger and with Obama's former mentor, Rev. Jeremiah Wright.

Trinity United Church of Christ's *Trumpet* news magazine honored Farrakhan in 2007 with the "Rev. Dr. Jeremiah A. Wright, Jr. Lifetime Achievement Trumpeteer" award, praising Farrakhan as someone who "truly epitomized greatness." *Washington Post* columnist Richard Cohen responded on January 15, 2008, saying, "For most Americans...Farrakhan epitomizes racism." [165] Cohen spoke with Obama campaign officials who, he wrote, declined to address the Farrakhan matter. That changed after Cohen's column hit the newsstands. An Obama statement suddenly appeared which read, "I decry racism and anti-Semitism in every form and strongly condemn the anti-Semitic statements made by Minister Farrakhan." The statement stopped short of denouncing Farrakhan himself.

Later, after Farrakhan endorsed Obama in February 2008, NBC's Tim Russert pressed Obama, during a debate with Hillary Clinton, asking "Do you accept the support of Louis Farrakhan?" and "Do you reject his support?" Obama was slow to issue an unequivocal answer. He sidestepped Russert, refusing to say he rejected Farrakhan's endorsement. Only after Clinton said she had rejected an endorsement from an anti-Semitic party in her run for the U.S. Senate from New York did Obama finally say he would "reject and denounce." [166]

Like Father Pfleger, Rev. Wright has showered Farrakhan with fulsome praise, saying, for example, that the Nation of Islam leader's "depth on analysis when it comes to the racial ills of this nation is astounding and eye opening. He brings a perspective that is helpful and honest." [167]

"Astounding and eye-opening" is apt. Here is Farrakhan in his own words:

- "You are wicked deceivers of the American people. You have sucked their blood. You are not real Jews, those of you that are not real Jews. You are the synagogue of Satan, and you have wrapped your tentacles around the U.S. government, and you are deceiving and sending this nation to hell. But I warn you in the name of Allah, you would be wise to leave me alone. But if you choose to crucify me, know that Allah will crucify you." [168]

- "Listen, Jewish people don't have no hands that are free of the blood of us [blacks]. They owned slave ships. They bought and sold us. They raped and robbed us." [169]

- "It is an act of mercy to white people that we end your world.... We must end your world and bring in a new world." [170]

- "A decree of death has been passed on America. The judgment of God has been rendered and she must be destroyed." [171]

Farrakhan has traveled abroad to meet with America's enemies in Libya, Iran, Iraq, Syria, and Sudan where he has castigated the U.S. as the "great Satan." Wright accompanied Farrakhan to Libya in 1984 to meet with dictator Muammar Qadhafi.

After Farrakhan met with Qadhafi in Libya in 1996, Qadhafi offered to spend $1 billion to underwrite a Farrakhan-led effort to lobby the U.S. government. Libya's state-controlled media quoted Qadhafi saying,

"Our confrontation with America was [previously] like a fight against a fortress from outside, and today [with the NOI alliance] we found a breach to enter into this fortress and confront it." [172]

DiscovertheNetworks.org reports that Farrakhan was quoted in an Iranian newspaper saying: "God will destroy America by the hands of the Muslims.... God will not give Japan or Europe the honor of bringing down the United States; this is an honor God will bestow upon Muslims." [173]

In 1995 Farrakhan organized the "Million-Man March," in Washington, DC, an event attended by Barack Obama who called it "a powerful demonstration of an impulse and need for African-American men to come together to recognize each other and affirm our rightful place in the society." [174]

To his credit, Obama also said that "cursing out white folks is not going to get the job done. Anti-Semitic and anti-Asian statements are not going to lift us up." [175] But whatever modest indirect criticism Obama may have sent Farrakhan's way did not keep him from working with Farrakhan and his associates as he started his political ascent in the 1990s.

Former Nation of Islam insider Dr. Vibert White Jr. told writer Ken Timmerman that Obama and Farrakhan had "an open line between them" on political and policy matters.

"Remember that for years, if you were a politician in Chicago, you had to have some type of relationship with Louis Farrakhan. You had to. If you didn't, you would be ostracized out of black Chicago," said White who held the Nation of Islam's top post under Farrakhan and broke with NOI in the mid '90s after nearly 25 years in the organization. White faced death threats after he wrote the book *Inside the Nation of Islam*, prompting him to leave Illinois to teach at the University of Central Florida. [176]

An unidentified former Obama insider told Aaron Klein, author of *The Manchurian Candidate*, that at least two Nation of Islam staffers were on Obama's staff in the early stages of his service as an Illinois state senator. The one-time insider, who wished to remain anonymous, said, "A key constituency for Obama was Hyde Park, where Farrakhan lives. To be successful politically in that area, you need to be involved with Farrakhan, since he's a strong power in the district." [177]

The verdict of Wright, Pfleger, and Farrakahan that America is a deeply racist nation is one shared by two key academic influences on Obama, Charles Ogletree and Derrick Bell.

Team Obama

15

The Harvard Guides

Charles Ogletree and Derrick Bell, Attacking White Oppressors

Harvard law professor Charles Ogletree has been a friend and mentor to both Barack and Michelle Obama for more than 20 years. Described by KeyWiki as a "hard core radical with roots in the Maoist influenced Black Panthers movement," Ogletree is a long-time advocate of reparations payments for the descendants of African slaves who served on the Obama presidential campaign's black advisory council. [178] He was also a debate coach for the Obama campaign.

In 2002, Ogletree and Cornel West co-chaired [179] the presidential exploration committee of Al Sharpton, someone he called an "articulate voice" who "will raise issues about criminal justice, immigration, and corporate greed that traditional politicians will not raise." [180] In 2005, Ogletree stood with three former Black Panther members in protest of attempts to reopen the investigation of the 1971 murder of a San Francisco police officer for which the three Black Panther members had been indicted by a grand jury. The three were later released after a court concluded that illegal means were used to obtain information about the crime.

Ogletree, who was editor of a Black Panthers

newspaper called *The Real News* while a student at Stanford University, said the three former Black Panthers "have been victims of the most vicious forms of American terrorism and torture" and vowed to protect them at all costs. "It takes a village to protect its elders. ...They will not come in this village and take these elders, except over our dead bodies." [181]

Others standing with Ogletree in defense of the ex-Black Panthers were actor Danny Glover, reparations payments advocate Ron Daniels, and Democratic Socialists of America member Bill Fletcher, Jr.

Ogletree said his "goal as a mentor [to Barack and Michelle] was simply to impart upon them not just the rudiments of the law but also the requirements of social justice and public service, and I've been very pleased to see the both of them engaging in that work." [182]

He also said he suppressed a video showing Barack praising and hugging Derrick Bell, a Harvard law professor who is the founder of "critical race theory" which holds that America's racial divide is a permanent split between white oppressors and black victims. In the video, Obama tells a 1991 campus rally that Bell is someone known for "speaking the truth" who has "opened up new vistas and new horizons" and "changed the standards [of what] legal writing is about." [183]

As he introduces Bell, Obama urges the crowd to "Open up your hearts and your minds to the words of Professor Derrick Bell." [184]

In his 1992 book, *Faces at the Bottom of the Well: The Permanence of Racism,* Bell wrote that racism is "an integral, permanent, and indestructible component of this society." He offered no hope for curing race hatred in America: "Black people will never gain full equality in this country.... African Americans must confront and conquer the otherwise deadening reality of our permanent subordinate status." Bell also praised Louis Farrakhan as someone who is "perhaps the best living example of a black man ready, willing and able to 'tell it like it is' regarding who is responsible for racism in this country." [185]

Along with video showing Obama praising Bell, Breitbart unearthed another video clip in which Ogletree proclaims, "We hid this throughout the 2008 campaign. I don't care if they find it now."[186] When that video came to light, Ogletree claimed he was only joking—it was a sarcastic comment made for comic effect. Whether that's true or not is quite open to question. What's certain is that before the 2008 election voters were not shown Obama praising a radical legal theorist who viewed whites as permanent oppressors.

Team Obama

16
Barack's PLO Babysitter

Rashid Khalidi, Anti-Semite, Obama's Friend

Barack Obama had nothing but kind words at a farewell dinner in 2003 for his long-time friend Rashid Khalidi and his wife Mona. Khalidi, whom Obama reportedly met at the University of Chicago where both taught, was leaving Chicago to become the Edward Said Professor of Arab Studies at Columbia University, a prestigious and influential post.

In his tribute Obama recalled many conversations with the Khalidis, which were, he said "consistent reminders to me of my own blind spots and my own biases.... It's for that reason that I'm hoping that, for many years to come, we continue that conversation — a conversation that is necessary not just around Mona and Rashid's dinner table," but around "this entire world." [187]

Also attending the dinner were Bill Ayers and Bernardine Dohrn. Ayers and Khalidi, Kurtz says, are "best friends," and the Obamas are close to the Khalidis, who have babysat the Obama's daughters.[188] Along with entertaining Barack and Michelle in their home, the Khalidis also organized a fundraiser for Obama when he unsuccessfully ran for Congress in 2000.

What makes this all so intriguing is that Khalidi,

according to writer Andrew McCarthy, is a "former mouthpiece for master terrorist Yasser Arafat." [189] Along with his professorial duties at Columbia, Khalidi also leads the school's Middle East studies program, which, McCarthy claims, "he has...maintained as a bubbling cauldron of anti-Semitism." [190]

Khalidi has denied working for the PLO but he was at times identified as a PLO spokesman in news reports from Beirut when he taught at the American University in Beirut from 1976 to 1983, a time when the PLO was designated as a terror group by the U.S. His wife, Mona, worked during that period for WAFA, the PLO's official news agency. Despite Khalidi's denials, Aaron Klein reports that "Palestinian diplomatic sources in Ramallah told WND [WorldNetDaily] he indeed worked on behalf of WAFA." [191] Khalidi later served, Klein writes, as an advisor to the Palestinian delegation to the Madrid Conference in 1991.

Khalidi is also tied to the PLO by his work as a writer for a journal published by the Institute for Palestine Studies, a research group in Beirut that claims to be independent but which, Klein writes, "functioned as the clear intellectual arm of the PLO from its foundation until the early 1990s. Many of its board members and featured authors were early pioneers of PLO ideology. [192]

In 1995, Khalidi co-founded with his wife, Mona, the Arab American Action Network, a Chicago-based group which has referred to Israel's creation as El Nakba, (the Catastrophe). Obama, while serving on the Woods Fund board, along with Bill Ayers, helped steer grants worth $75,000 to the AAAN.

A bitter critic of Israel, Khalidi has called the Jewish

state an "apartheid system in creation" and a "racist" state. Khalidi supplied a justification in 2002 for killing Israeli soldiers. Speaking to the American-Arab Anti-Discrimination Committee, Khalidi said:

> Killing civilians is a war crime. It's a violation of international law. They are not soldiers. They're civilians, they're unarmed. The ones who are armed, the ones who are soldiers, the ones who are in occupation, that's different. That's resistance.[193]

Klein reports that Khalidi "has multiple times expressed support for Palestinian terror, calling suicide bombings a response to 'Israeli aggression.'" [194]

Comments like that prompted the New York City schools chancellor to drop Khalidi from a program to train teachers on how to teach about the Middle East. "Considering his past statements," a missive from the chancellor's office read, "Rashid Khalidi should not have been included in a program that provided professional development for DOE teachers and he won't be participating in the future." [195]

Too extreme for New York city teachers, Khalidi can take comfort in knowing he has the ear of the President of the United States. Khalidi, who endorsed Obama for president in 2008 "because he is the only candidate who has expressed sympathy for the Palestinian cause," [196] can look forward, as Obama put it in his 2003 farewell dinner tribute, to continuing conversations that further expose "my own blind spots and my own biases."

17

The Wife And Chicago Ideologue

Michelle Obama, Marching To Barack's Left

"By any measure," says Edward Klein, author of *The Amateur*, "Michelle Obama is further to the Left politically than her husband. And that's saying a lot." [197]

A former Obama presidential campaign adviser calls her "very much the Chicago ideologue" and suggests she "might be to the left of Nancy Pelosi"—and *that* is saying a lot.

"She really doesn't care for how things work in the country and she wants to see it all changed," according to this former campaign worker. "I can respect that, though I would guess she is far too liberal even for me – and I consider myself a liberal Democrat." [198]

All this matters because, as Klein states, "Michelle is the president's most important political adviser and the one he listens to above all others before he makes major decisions."

It was her advice, Klein writes, that helped persuade Obama to disregard White House advisers like Rahm Emanuel, David Axelrod, and Vice President Joe

Biden who argued for a take-it-slow approach to health care reform legislation. Instead, "Michelle encouraged her husband's messianic impulses, urging him to save America from its wicked ways and press ahead, no matter what the consequences." [199] Michelle Robinson grew up on Chicago's South Side, the daughter of a city worker and Democrat precinct captain, and a stay-at-home mom. She did well in school and made it into Princeton and Harvard Law School. One of her mentors at Harvard was Charles Ogletree, a law professor who also mentored Barack when he studied at Harvard. The mentorship has continued, according to Ogletree, who says that both Barack and Michelle "have not hesitated to call on me over the past 20-plus years as needed." [200]

After graduating from Harvard, Michelle returned to work in Chicago at a law firm where Bernardine Dohrn also worked. She moved on from there to work for Chicago Mayor Richard Daley, as a nonprofit director, and for the University of Chicago Hospitals where she earned a salary of $316,962 in 2005.

She and Barack prospered, reporting 2007 income of $4,139,965 and $2,656,902 the year after. Despite living the American dream, Michelle served up a campaign stump speech offering a grim assessment of life in these United States. She told a crowd in March 2008 that the U.S. is "just downright mean" as a nation. "We have become a nation of struggling folks who are barely making it every day," she told South Carolinians. "Folks are just jammed up, and it's gotten worse over my lifetime." [201]

Her discontent with America wasn't just over economics. Race was a frequent subtext as when she announced at a February 18, 2008, campaign stop in Milwaukee, "For the first time in my adult lifetime,

I am really proud of my country, and not just because Barack has done well, but because I think people are hungry for change." [202]

She implied on the CBS *60 Minutes* program that white racism posed a real threat to her husband, telling interviewer Steve Kroft, "As a black man, you know, Barack can get shot going to the gas station." [203] (Some 8,000 to 9,000 black men are murdered each year with about 93 percent of these crimes perpetrated by other blacks). [204]

Michelle's sense of racial grievance is front and center in her Princeton thesis, "Princeton-Educated Blacks and the Black Community," which includes these remarkable claims:

- "Predominately white universities like Princeton are socially and academically designed to cater to the needs of the white students comprising the bulk of their enrollments."

- "[My Princeton experiences], will likely lead to my further integration and/or assimilation into a White cultural and social structure that will only allow me to remain on the periphery of society; never becoming a full participant."

- "I have found that at Princeton, no matter how liberal and open-minded some of my white professors and classmates try to be toward me, I sometimes feel like a visitor on campus; as if I really don't belong. Regardless of the circumstances under which I interact with whites at Princeton, it often seems as if, to them, I will always be black first and a student second." [205]

While her background is nowhere near as exotic as her husband's, Michelle has a resume that rivals his for involvement in the world of community organizing. She helped train organizers as an original faculty member of the Asset-Based Community Development Institute, a community organizing institute at Northwestern co-founded by Obama mentor John McKnight, who recommended Barack to Harvard.

With Barack's backing, Michelle became the founding executive director in 1993 of Public Allies, a leadership development group in Chicago that groomed future community activists and organizers through 10-month apprenticeships with other non-profit organizations. Led by Michelle, Public Allies became a "training and recruitment funnel into the Midwest Academy network," says Kurtz,[206] who calls the Academy a "socialist front." After stepping down as executive director in 1996, Michelle served on the Public Allies national board of directors from 1997 until 2001.

Public Allies was, effectively, an extension of the Midwest Academy, a community organizer training institute founded in 1973 by a group that included former SDS leader Paul Booth, and his activist wife Heather Booth. Pledged to "advancing the struggle for social, economic, and racial justice," the Midwest Academy claims it has trained more than 30,000 activists in "progressive organizations, unions, and faith-based groups" since its founding.

With its links to ACORN, Public Allies, and other groups in the Chicago socialist orbit, the Midwest Academy is a major player in modern American socialism, and one to which the Obamas are closely linked. Kurtz calls it "arguably the most influential institutional force in community organizing from the seventies through the nineties, and very much a crypto-socialist organization." [207]

Still largely unknown, "the Midwest Academy's history, cast of characters, and organizational reach are at least as extensive as ACORN's," says Kurtz, who concludes that "both Barack and Michelle Obama have close and longstanding ties to a thoroughly socialist network of community organizers, politicians, and political activists centered on the Midwest Academy." [208]

So what is the Midwest Academy and what are its goals for America?

Team Obama

18
The Midwest Academy

Revolution By The Inch

M idwest Academy co-founder Heather Booth was in a celebratory mood a month after Barack Obama's inauguration. Speaking to a group in Washington, D.C., she credited community organizing with being a primary factor that "brought us to this extraordinary moment."

"There is an opening for change that is precious," said Booth. "We have not had a time like this for 40 years." But, she cautioned, "We can only make the change promised by this moment—the positive change—if we organize." [209]

That Booth so clearly linked the arrival of America's transformative moment to the work of community organizing brings the electoral agenda of her organization, the Midwest Academy, into sharp focus.

That agenda goes back to 1969 when a small group, including Heather Booth; her husband Paul, a SDS national secretary; Steve Max, former SDS field secretary; and radical Harry Boyte published "Socialism and the Coming Decade." The pamphlet counseled against violence to achieve the longed-for revolution and advocated, as Discoverthe Networks.org reports, a "stealth, incremental approach to social change. It further advised community organizations to agitate for concrete issues like urban redevelopment and health care, thereby giving 'the socialist movement relevance to the daily lives of the people.'" [210]

That approach—revolution by the inch via community organizing and using Alinskyite tactics— became the blueprint for change at the Midwest Academy, the training institute founded in 1973 in Chicago by Heather Booth and Steve Max. It was also the model for change in which the young community organizer Barack Obama was trained, as Kurtz notes:

> The Midwest Academy succeeded in synthe-
> sizing the community organizing techniques of
> Saul Alinsky with the sort of national electoral
> strategy Alinsky had long refused to
> countenance. Through their vision, ambition,
> and ideological earnestness, the leaders of the
> Midwest Academy turned Alinsky's localized
> techniques into the key to an ambitious
> national strategy of socialist transformation.
> Barack Obama, by all accounts a brilliant
> student of community organizing, was for years
> in an ideal position to drink all of this in. [211]

But even though the path forward was gradual and cloaked in stealth, socialism remained the goal. Among the objectives laid out in the 1969 document was a guaranteed annual salary for every American. And if violence became necessary to bring about change, Heather Booth was apparently willing in 1975 to take that shortcut: "Truly reaching socialism or feminism," she said, "will likely take a revolution that is in fact violent, a rupture with the old ways in which the current ruling class and elites are wiped out." [212]

The Midwest Academy created a "Committee of Correspondence" in 1977 to facilitate more candid communication between community organizers about their work and their goals. Kurtz obtained access to Midwest Academy archives which contain some of that correspondence, including this note from an unnamed writer from Washington, D.C., on the importance of stealth: "If we initially start out by talking about reallocating wealth and power, let alone about 'socialism,' we will turn too many people off to build the kind of socialist mass movement we seek." [213]

Kurtz calls the Midwest Academy "the hidden key to Barack Obama's political career." Nearly all of the individuals and entities that influenced or funded his work as a community organizer have some link back to the Midwest Academy.

The late Marxist intellectual Manning Marable said "A lot of the people working with him [Obama] are, indeed, socialists with backgrounds in the Communist Party or as independent Marxists." Add to that comment the fact that most of them are linked in some way to the Midwest Academy. Thanks to the research of Kurtz, the links have been exposed. Let's take a quick look.

Ken Rolling—A top administrator for the Midwest Academy, Rolling worked with Obama in various ways for 15 years. He helped fund Barack Obama's work as a community organizer, worked with him on the Woods Fund, and ran the Chicago Annenberg Challenge under Obama and Ayers. [214]

Harry Boyte—A socialist theorist who co-authored a 1969 document which rejected violence in favor of a stealthy, step-by-step approach to moving America toward socialism—the approach adopted by the Midwest Academy. Obama read Boyte's work and Boyte advised the 2008 Obama presidential campaign.[215]

John Cameron—An official at the Illinois Public Action Council, which was, Kurtz writes, "effectively the Midwest Academy's action arm."[216] Cameron, author of *"A Socialist's Guide to Citizen Action,"* worked with Obama when he was in the Illinois Senate.

William McNary—Illinois Public Action Council legislative director who is also linked to Democratic Socialists of America. Had close friendship and political partnership with Obama.[217] "Barack was not just willing to meet with community-based groups, not only to be a good vote for us," said McNary, "but he also strategized with us to help move our position forward."[218]

Lane Evans—Recruited by IPAC to run for Congress in 1982, he modeled Harry Boyte's concept of a "successful synergy between grassroots organizing and national politics."[219] He addressed Midwest Academy retreats. Endorsed Obama for Senate in 2004 and was in Obama's hotel room on Election Night, 2008.

Alice Palmer—Socialist sympathizer who worked with Ken Rolling at Midwest Academy and endorsed Obama for her seat in the Illinois Senate.

Heather Booth—Midwest Academy co-founder, Booth served on the founding board of Public Allies with Obama and joined in hiring Michelle Obama as Public Allies' first executive director. Lobbied heavily for passage of Obama-backed Dodd-Frank bill and gushed over Obama as "this extraordinary President."

Greg Galluzzo and Mary Gonzales—Galluzzo was an early Obama mentor who did organizing work for the Illinois Public Action Council, the Midwest Academy's action arm. Gonzales, Galluzzo's wife, served on board of Citizen Action, an advocacy group heavily influenced by the Midwest Academy.

Jackie Kendall—Executive director of Midwest Academy from 1982 to 2010, Kendall met Obama in mid-1980s. She served on the founding board of Public Allies with Barack Obama and helped present "Camp Obama" trainings for Obama campaign volunteers in Iowa.

Robert Creamer—Member of Midwest Academy's founding board and one-time executive director of the Midwest Academy-spawned IPAC, Creamer is the author of the influential book, *Stand Up Straight! How Progressives Can Win*, which Obama advisor David Axelrod called a "blueprint for future victories." Creamer also worked as a Camp Obama instructor.

John McKnight—Northwestern University professor who trained Obama in community organizing and recommended Obama to Harvard Law School. McKnight helped recruit students to Midwest Academy and co-founded the organizing institute at which Michelle Obama served as an original faculty member.

Jacky Grimshaw—Midwest Academy board member who recommended Obama to lead Project VOTE!, Grimshaw is a next-door Chicago neighbor of the Obamas and member of the founding board of Public Allies with Barack and Heather Booth.

Rahm Immanuel—Chicago mayor, Immanuel is

Obama's former White House Chief of Staff who once served as finance director of the Midwest Academy-linked Illinois Public Action Council.

Obama's many links to the Midwest Academy offer a powerful clue to his ideology and strategic vision for achieving what he has called "Hope and Change," and now "Forward," both code for implementing a socialist transformation of America.

The Midwest Academy model of synthesizing a stealthy, incremental socialism powered by community organizing, and an electoral and legislative strategy heavily informs the approach to politics adopted by our current president. A socialist front group's philosophy for social change is the template being followed by the leader of capitalist (heretofore) America. Lessons learned and strategies refined in Chicago are being followed in Washington today.

19
Obama's Narrator

David Axelrod, Mentored by Radicals

H is mother wrote in the 1940s for a left-leaning newspaper with links to the Communist Party. He was mentored while in college by a left-leaning journalist/activist and by a paid Soviet propagandist who spent part of his youth in the Soviet Union.

Those facts are not usually included in the glowing profiles to which Obama adviser David Axelrod has become accustomed.

If Karl Rove was the Architect, Axelrod is the Narrator of the Obama story and, likely, Obama's number one fan. After all, Axelrod's nickname for Obama is "black Jesus."

"I do love Barack Obama," Axelrod told the Public Broadcasting Service in 2008. "I believe in him. I think he's an extraordinary person." [220]

He says they are ideological twins. "You know, he and I share a basic worldview ... I trust his basic take on what the country should be and where we need to move towards." [221]

A political junkie from an early age, Axelrod grew up on New York's Lower East Side and attended the University of Chicago while also working as a reporter for the *Hyde Park Herald*. He later wrote for the

Chicago Tribune and jumped into the world of political consulting in 1984, meeting Barack Obama in 1992.

Axelrod grew up in a liberal household. His mother, Myril Bennett, worked in the 1940s for *PM* magazine, a left-leaning publication that had on its staff numerous writers with ties to Communist groups. New Zealand blogger Trevor Loudon has noted that:

> Former Communist Eugene Lyons, writing in *The Red Decade: The Stalinist Penetration of America*, noted that *PM's* staff included a former editor of the *Daily Worker*; another was former editor of *The Communist*; a third was a leader of the Communist Youth League; a fourth was a Soviet government official; and a fifth was the former staff cartoonist for the *Daily Worker*, the official newspaper of the Communist Party, USA.[222]

Journalist I.F. Stone who was, Loudon writes, "later identified as involved in Soviet Intelligence operations," served as *PM's* Washington, D.C. correspondent.[223]

While attending the University of Chicago and writing for the *Hyde Park Herald* in the mid-1970s, Axelrod came to know Don Rose and the late David Canter, left-wing activists with Communist ties who mentored the young journalist. Canter and Rose were co-publishers of the *Hyde Park-Kenwood Voices*, which adopted a pro-Communist tilt, campaigning, for example, against the House Committee on Un-American Activities.

Rose described the mentoring relationship he and

Canter had with Axelrod in a letter to Canter's son, Marc Canter:

> Just for the historical record, David Axelrod did not work for the *Voices* at any point. He was a reporter for the *HP Herald* while attending U of C, appearing on the scene first in 1975, just after the *Voices* folded— but he was familiar with our paper as a student before he got the *Herald* job. Your dad and I "mentored" and helped educate him politically in that capacity, which is perhaps why you may recall seeing him hanging around the house. I later wrote a reference letter for him that helped him win an internship at the *Tribune*, which was the next step in his journalism career. [224]

KeyWiki.com reports that Rose, a Chicago journalist and socialist activist, has a history of radical activism that goes back to the 1940s when he joined Henry Wallace's Communist-controlled Progressive Party. Rose took part in the nuclear disarmament campaign in the 1950s, became involved in the civil rights movement in the 1960s, and with the National Mobilization Committee to End the War in Vietnam in 1968. [225] In the late 1970s Rose was a part of a coalition of "former Trotskyists, Socialist Party USA members and communists that would in 1982 form Democratic Socialists of America." [226]

David Canter (1923-2004) was a "red-diaper baby" whose father, Harry, served as secretary of the Boston Communist Party USA and was invited in 1932 to live in Soviet Russia where the family spent five years. "The family was invited to go over to the Soviet Union so that my grandfather could teach printing techniques to the Russians," said Harry's grandson

Evan, son of David. "They were translating ideological papers into English at that time. I have several volumes of translated works that he printed, including a series of Lenin's translated papers that actually have my grandfather's name in them." [227]

Canter and Communist Party USA member LeRoy Wolins owned *Translation World Publishers*, which specialized in publications from and about the Soviet Union. After investigating *World Publishers*, the House Committee on Un-American Activities concluded that:

> *Translation World Publishers* was an outlet for the distribution of Soviet propaganda...this publishing house was subsidized by Soviet funds and was created by known Communists to serve the propaganda interests of the USSR. [228]

Canter appeared before the Committee but refused to answer the charge that he was a Communist Party member brought under oath by former Party member Carl Nelson. [229]

Loudon writes that Canter was a "key Chicago political fixer who helped elect communist linked politicians including the late Chicago mayor Harold Washington and former U.S. Senator Carol Moseley Braun." [230]

Both Rose and Axelrod served on Harold Washington's mayoral campaign, Rose as an adviser to Washington and Axelrod as a campaign consultant. [231] Trevor Loudon reports that, along with Canter, Rose and Axelrod "played senior roles in the successful campaign," of Carol Mosely Braun for U.S. Senate while Barack Obama "ran the highly successful voter registration drive," Project VOTE!, that "secured Moseley Braun's victory." [232]

Axelrod produced a film project on renegade priest Father Michael Pfleger and raised funds to repair his church. In 2000, Axelrod initiated a documentary on Father Pfleger that became the 2009 video *Radical Disciple: The Story of Father Pfleger*. The film profiles Pfleger's work at St. Sabina, including his gun-control crusade, his work to clear the streets of prostitutes, and his opposition to porn and tobacco. It includes footage of Pfleger's guest sermon at Rev. Wright's church mocking Hillary Clinton.

Axelrod, who is Jewish, has helped raise funds for Father Michael Pfleger's St. Sabina Catholic Church. He served on the church finance board, as it sought to raise $1 million for church repairs.

Obama's chief political strategist is connected as well to Midwest Academy founding board member Robert Creamer, having endorsed Creamer's book, *Stand Up Straight! How Progressives Can Win*, as a "blueprint for future victories." Axelrod wrote a letter of recommendation for Creamer when he was to be sentenced in 2006 for tax evasion and bank fraud.

Given his radical mentors, Don Rose and David Canter, is Axelrod a communist at heart? That's unknown, but as historian Paul Kengor says, such mentors "are formative to Axelrod's life and political rise, and cannot be ignored."

Kengor, author of the new book, *The Communist: Frank Marshall Davis, The Untold Story of Barack Obama's Mentor,* believes these mentors reveal that:

> Axelrod—just like Barack Obama—is the product of some far-left influences, from the progressive left to the communist left. Like Obama, who was impacted by Frank Marshall

Davis, Bill Ayers, Jeremiah Wright, and others, these figures unquestionably had an impact and surely help explain why Axelrod is on the left—and not the moderate left. [233]

20
Only in Chicago

America's Second City, a Long Communist Presence

Amerca's second city has long had a communist presence. In fact, it goes back to the 19th century. The *New York Times* reported in 1880 that "Chicago is the center of the Socialistic organizations." [234]

The *Times* carried this troubling notice on April 25, 1878: "The Police report that the communist element here [Chicago] already numbers several thousands, and that many drilling places are almost nightly frequented by armed men." [235] Another dispatch a year later, April 21, 1879, told readers that, "About 1100 Communists paraded the streets to-day, and displayed inflammatory banners. About 400 of them were armed. No disturbance occurred." [236]

It was in Chicago that the American Communist Party came into existence in September 1919. After that, the city quickly became a distribution point for Communist ideas. "Chicago has been one of the chief radiating centers for Communist propaganda in the United States," Harold Lasswell and Dorothy Blumenstock wrote in 1939. While Communist Party headquarters moved to New York in 1924, Chicago, they wrote, "has always remained a stronghold of the party." [237]

Historian Paul Kengor writes that Chicago in the 1930s was the "heart of the American Communist Party, second only to New York in Party activity." [238]

It was in Chicago that Frank Marshall Davis linked up with communist front groups, including the Abraham Lincoln School, which gave students lessons on Marx and Lenin. Davis joined the American Communist Party in 1943, and was given Communist Party card number 47544.

And it was to Chicago that young Obama decamped in 1985, determined to make his mark as a community organizer.

What he found in the Windy City made all the difference in his life—and in the life of the nation.

Marilyn Katz, one of the many Leftists with whom Obama rubbed shoulders in Chicago, said Obama's political ascent could not have taken place anywhere else. Katz was an SDS leader in the 1960s who, the *New York Times* reports, "organized Vietnam War protests, throwing nails in the street to thwart the police" [239] and also served as the SDS "security chief" during the 1968 Chicago riots.

She thinks Obama's rise would not have happened without the critical mass of people on the Left with whom he was surrounded. While communist influence in Chicago long predates events in 1968, the growth of a socialist network, Katz says, began at the Chicago Democratic Convention during which student riots were put down by Chicago police.

My straight line goes from '66/'68 to the folks who began to work together and formed the core

group of the Harold Washington campaign.
(Almost) everyone I worked with in 1982 I had
met as a kid in '68. I believe that Barack Obama
could only have emerged in Chicago. Why?
Because since '68 there was a web of relationships
between black civil rights groups, anti-war groups,
women's activities, immigrant rights activities, that
has sustained and grown. [240]

That web of friendships formed a socialists-
friendly culture into which Obama entered with
ease. His long background on the left, starting
with his liberal parents and grandparents, and
moving on to his communist mentor Frank
Marshall Davis and his Marxist-Leninist stance
in college, all prepared him for what he found
in Chicago. It was what he was looking for—
and it made him what he is today: A stealth
socialist eager to use organizing to advance his
radical agenda.

It's the Chicago Way. But, please God, may it never
be the American Way.

Endnotes

1. Manning Marable, "The four legged stool that won the US presidential election," Socialist Review, December 2008, http:// www.socialistreview.org.uk/ article.php? articlenumber = 10628. Emphasis in original. Quoted in Klein, Aaron; Elliott, Brenda J. (2010-03-05). The Manchurian President (p. 315). Midpoint Trade Books. Kindle Edition.

2. Klein, Edward (2012-05-14). The Amateur (p. 15). Perseus Books Group. Kindle Edition.

3. David Whelan, "Obama's Doctor Knocks ObamaCare," Forbes, June 18, 2009. http://www.forbes.com/2009/06/18/obama-doctor-knocks-obamacare-business-healthcare-obamas-doctor.html

4. Physicians for a National Health Program, KeyWiki.org, http://keywiki.org/index.php/Physicians_for_a_National_Health_Program#cite_note-1

5. Ben Smith, "Obama once visited '60s radicals," Politico, Feb. 22, 2008. http://www.politico.com/news/stories/0208/8630.html

6. Kurtz, Stanley (2010-10-19). Radical-in-Chief (p. 12). Simon & Schuster, Inc.. Kindle Edition.

7. Radical-in-Chief (p. 17).

8. Linda Matchen, "A Law Review Breakthrough", Boston Globe 15 Feb 1990, p. 29. Quoted in Bragg, William Washington (2011-09-07). Obama's Radical Roots: Saul Alinsky, Jeremiah Wright, and the Others who Shaped his Worldview (Kindle Locations 2183-2184). Jefferson Adams Library of American History. Kindle Edition.

9. Obama, Barack (2007-01-09). Dreams from My Father: A Story of Race and Inheritance (Kindle Location 1012). Random House, Inc.. Kindle Edition.

10. D'Souza, Dinesh (2011-10-03). The Roots of Obama's Rage (p. 74). Perseus Books Group. Kindle Edition.

11. Ibid.

12. Obama, Barack (2007-01-09). Dreams from My Father: A Story of Race and Inheritance (Kindle Location 197). Random House, Inc.. Kindle Edition. Quoted in D'Souza, Dinesh (2011-10-03). The Roots of Obama's Rage (p. 26). Perseus Books Group. Kindle Edition.

13. D'Souza, Dinesh (2011-10-03). The Roots of Obama's Rage (p. 34). Perseus Books Group. Kindle Edition.

14. Ibid.

15. Barak H. Obama, "Problems Facing Our Socialism," East Africa Journal, July 1965.

16. D'Souza, Dinesh (2011-10-03). The Roots of Obama's Rage (p. 36). Perseus Books Group. Kindle Edition.

17. Tim Jones, "Barack Obama: Mother not just a girl from Kansas," Chicago Tribune, March 27, 2007. http://www.chicagotribune.com/news/politics/obama/c hi-0703270151mar27-archive,0,5853572,full.story

18. Obama, Barack (2007-01-09). Dreams from My Father: A Story of Race and Inheritance (Kindle Location 1005). Random House, Inc.. Kindle Edition.

19. Jonathan Martin, "Obama's mother known here as 'uncommon,'" The Seattle Times, April 8, 2008. http://seattletimes.nwsource.com/html/politics/200433 4057_obama08m.html

20. "East Shore History," East Shore Unitarian Church. http://www.eastshoreunitarian.org/index.php?option=c om_content&view=article&id=82&Itemid=99.

21. Tim Jones, "Barack Obama: Mother not just a girl from Kansas," Chicago Tribune, March 27, 2007. http://www.chicagotribune.com/news/politics/obama/c hi-0703270151mar27-archive,0,5853572,full.story

22. Mary Adamski, "A Time for Peace," Honolulu Star-Bulletin, February 8, 2003, http://archives.starbulletin.com/2003/02/08/features/st ory1.html

23. Obama, Barack (2007-01-09). Dreams from My Father: A Story of Race and Inheritance (Kindle Locations 457-461). Random House, Inc.. Kindle Edition.

24. Obama, Barack (2007-01-09). Dreams from My Father: A Story of Race and Inheritance (Kindle Locations 1457-1465). Random House, Inc.. Kindle Edition.

25. Frank Marshall Davis, Livin' the Blues: Memoirs of a Black Journalist Poet (Madison, WI: University of Wisconsin Press, 1992), 243. Quoted in Kengor, Paul (2010-12-15). Dupes: How America's Adversaries Have Manipulated Progressives for a Century (Kindle Locations 5281-5283). ISI Books. Kindle Edition.

26. Frank Marshall Davis, Keywiki entry. http://keywiki.org/index.php/Frank_Marshall_Davis

27. "I am at home," Daily Worker, January 15, 1935. http:// www.marxists.org/archive/robeson/1935/01/15.htm

28. Frank Marshall Davis, KeyWiki.com. http://keywiki.org/index.php/Frank_Marshall_Davis

29. Jack Cashill, "Time and Again, Maraniss Conceals

Obama's Socialist Roots," AmericanThinker.com, June 26, 2012. http://www.americanthinker.com/2012/06 /time_and_again_maraniss_conceals_obamas_socialist _roots.html

30. Toby Harnden, "Frank Marshall Davis, alleged Communist, was early influence on Barack Obama," The Telegraph, August 22, 2008. http://www.telegraph.co.uk /news/worldnews/barackobama/2601914/Frank-Marshall-Davis-alleged-Communist-was-early-influenc e-on-Barack-Obama.html

31. Ibid.

32. Obama, Barack (2007-01-09). Dreams from My Father: A Story of Race and Inheritance (Kindle Locations 1713-1715). Random House, Inc.. Kindle Edition.

33. Obama, Dreams from My Father, (Kindle Locations 1812-1814).

34. Obama, Dreams from My Father (Kindle Locations 1813-1818).

35. Obama, Dreams from My Father (Kindle Location 1872-75).

36. Janny Scott, 'Obama's Account of New York Years Often Differs From What Others Say," New York Times, October 30, 2007. http://www.nytimes.com/2007/10/30/us/politics/30ob ama.html?_r=2&pagewanted=all

37. Paul Kengor, "Obama's Missing Link," American-Thinker.com, December 10, 2010. http://www.americanthinker.com/2010/12/obamas_mi ssing_link_1.html

38. John C. Drew, "Meeting Young Obama," American-Thinker.com, February 27, 2012. http://www. american thinker.com/2011/02/meeting_young_obama.html

39. Obama, Barack (2007-01-09). Dreams from My Father: A Story of Race and Inheritance (Kindle Locations 1964-1969). Random House, Inc.. Kindle Edition.

40. Jim Tranquada, "Barack Obama '83 Elected President," Occidental College, November4, 2008, http:// www.oxy.edu/ x8270. xml. Klein, Aaron; Elliott, Brenda J. (2010-03-05). The Manchurian President (p. 277). Midpoint Trade Books. Kindle Edition.

41. Barack Obama, ""Breaking the War Mentality," Sun Dial, March 10, 1983. http://graphics8.nytimes.com/packages/images/nytint/ docs/obama-s-1983-college-magazine-article/original.pdf

42. Obama, Barack (2007-01-09). Dreams from My Father: A Story of Race and Inheritance (Kindle Locations 2383-2386). Random House, Inc.. Kindle Edition.

43. Kurtz, Stanley (2010-10-19). Radical-in-Chief (pp. 4-5). Simon & Schuster, Inc.. Kindle Edition.

44. Kurtz, Stanley (2010-10-19). Radical-in-Chief (p. 4). Simon & Schuster, Inc.. Kindle Edition.

45. Cornel West, "Review of How Capitalism Underdeveloped Black America," Guardian Book Supplement, Summer 1984, p. 5. Quoted in Kurtz, Stanley (2010-10-19). Radical-in-Chief (p. 403). Simon & Schuster, Inc.. Kindle Edition.

46. Manning Marable, "The four legged stool that won the US presidential election," Socialist Review, December 2008, http:// www.socialistreview.org.uk/ article.php? articlenumber = 10628. Emphasis in original. Quoted in Klein, Aaron; Elliott, Brenda J. (2010-03-05). The Manchurian President (p. 315). Midpoint Trade Books. Kindle Edition.

47. L. David Alinsky, "Son sees father's handiwork in convention," Boston Globe, August 31, 2008. http://www.boston.com/bostonglobe/editorial_opinion/letters/articles/2008/08/31/son_sees_fathers_handiwork_in_convention/

48. Saul Alinsky, Rules for Radicals (Random House, 1971), p. xxii.

49. Ibid., p. 116.

50. Ibid., p. 3.

51. Nicholas von Hoffman, Radical: A Portrait of Saul Alinsky Nation Books, 2010 p. 83-4. Quoted in Wikipedia, http://en.wikipedia.org/wiki/Saul_alinsky

52. Alinsky, p. ix.

53. Alinsky, p. 117.

54. Ryan Lizza, "The Agitator: Barack Obama's unlikely political education," The New Republic, March 19, 2007. http://www.discoverthenetworks.org/Articles/bobamasunlikelypoliticaledu.html.

55. Ibid.

56. Kurtz, Stanley (2010-10-19). Radical-in-Chief . Simon & Schuster, Inc.. Kindle Edition.

57. Gerald Kellman, DiscovertheNetworks.org, a Guide to the Political Left. http://www.discoverthenetworks.org/individualProfile.asp?indid=2548

58. Phil Davidson, "Obama's Mentor," Illinois Issues, March 2009. http://illinoisissues.uis.edu/archives/2009/03/kellman.html

59. "Q&A: Jodi Kantor," Texas Book Festival. http://www.texasbookfestival.org/Jodi_Kantor_Interview.php, emphasis added.

60. Daniel Libit, "The End of Community Organizing in Chicago?" Chicago Magazine, April 2011. http://www.chicagomag.com/Chicago-Magazine/April-2011/The-

End-of-Community-Organizing-in-Chicago/

61. Gregory Galluzzo, "Gamaliel and the Barack Obama Connection," http://web.archive.org/web/20090303170002/http://www.gamaliel.org/Obama%20Gamalie%20lConnection.htm

62. Kurtz, Stanley (2010-10-19). Radical-in-Chief (p. 96). Simon & Schuster, Inc.. Kindle Edition.

63. David Hogberg, "The Gamaliel Foundation: Alinsky-Inspired Group Uses Stealth Tactics to Manipulate Church Congregations," Foundation Watch, July 2010, The Capital Research Institute. http://www.capitalresearch.org/pubs/pdf/v1278370073.pdf

64. "John McKnight on Mentoring Barack Obama," Youtube video at 1:20. http://www.youtube.com/watch?v=UKsFpwlxPrI

65. Kurtz, Stanley (2010-10-19). Radical-in-Chief (p. 125). Simon & Schuster, Inc.. Kindle Edition.

66. Ibid., p. 146.

67. Ibid., p. 306.

68. Bill Ayers, Discover the Networks, http://www.discoverthenetworks.org/individualProfile.asp?indid=2169

69. Bill Ayers, Fugitive Days: Memoirs of an Anti-War Activist (Boston: Beacon Press, 2001), p. 264.

70. Ibid., p. 294.

71. Ibid., p. 295

72. Weather Underground, Conservapedia, http://www.conservapedia.com/Weather_Underground

73. "FBI Agent Talking About Bill Ayers," YouTube video, starting at 1:23. http://www.youtube.com/watch?v=tRg9il_V328

74. Bernardine Dohrn, Conservapedia, http://www.conservapedia.com/Bernardine_Dohrn

75. Bill Ayers, DiscovertheNetworks.org, http://www.discoverthenetworks.org/individualProfile.asp?indid=2169

76. The Real Story of the Weathermen - ties to the Cuban DGI," YouTube video at :30. http://www.youtube.com/watch?v=PI_hPDpOVTE&feature=related

77. Danita Smith, "No Regrets for a Love Of Explosives; In a Memoir of Sorts, a War Protester Talks of Life With the Weathermen," New York Times, September 11, 2001. http://www.nytimes.com/2001/09/11/books/no-regrets-for-love-explosives-memoir-sorts-war-protester-talks-life-with.html

78. Sol Stern, "The Bomber as School Reformer," City Journal, October 6, 2008, Emphasis added. Quoted in Klein, Aaron; Elliott, Brenda J. (2010-03-05). The Manchurian President (p. 212). Midpoint Trade Books. Kindle Edition.

79. David Remnick, The Bridge: The Life and Rise of
    Barack Obama, p. 280. Quoted in Kurtz, Stanley
    (2010-10-19). Radical-in-Chief (p. 318). Simon &
    Schuster, Inc.. Kindle Edition.

80. Chicago Annenberg Challenge, Discover the Networks,
    http://www.discoverthenetworks.org/groupProfile.asp?g
    rpid=7644

81. http://web.archive.org/web/20020922153719/www.
    chi-challenge.org/implement3.htm

82. Mark A. Smylie et al., "The Chicago Annenberg
    Challenge: Successes, Failures, and Lessons for the
    Future," Consortium on Chicago School Research,
    August 2003, pp. 98, 104. Quoted in Kurtz, Stanley
    (2010-10-19). Radical-in-Chief (p. 287). Simon &
    Schuster, Inc.. Kindle Edition.

83. Kurtz, Radical-in-Chief, p. 290.

84. Ibid., p. 327.

85. Christopher Andersen, Barack and Michelle: Portrait of
    a Marriage (New York: William Morrow, 2009), p. 165.

86. Ben Smith, "Obama once visited '60s radicals,"
    Politico.com, February 22, 2008.
    http://www.politico.com/news/stories/0208/8630.html

87. Midwest Academy, KeyWiki.org,
    http://keywiki.org/index.php/Midwest_Academy

88. Kurtz, Stanley (2010-10-19). Radical-in-Chief (p.
    189). Simon & Schuster, Inc.. Kindle Edition.

89. Alice Palmer, KeyWiki.org,
    http://keywiki.org/index.php/Alice_Palmer

90. Ibid.

91. Ibid.

92. Alice Palmer, Discoverthenetworks.org,
    http://www.discoverthenetworks.org/individualProfile.a
    sp?indid=2325

93. Kurtz, Stanley (2010-10-19). Radical-in-Chief (p.
    214). Simon & Schuster, Inc.. Kindle Edition.

94. Klein, Aaron; Elliott, Brenda J. (2010-03-05). The
    Manchurian President (p. 82). Midpoint Trade Books.
    Kindle Edition.

95. New Party Principles, http://thirdworldtraveler.com/
    Political/NewParty_Principles.html

96. Kurtz, Stanley (2010-10-19). Radical-in-Chief (p.
    239). Simon & Schuster, Inc.. Kindle Edition. Note in
    Kurtz indicates that "The Cantor/ Rogers proposal is
    quoted in a letter/ memo from Jim Lardner titled
    'MORE THAN A PARTY,' ACORN Records, 1973–
    1997, Box 1, Folder: New Party (one of several
    similarly titled folders)."

97. Barack Obama and the New Party/Progressive Chicago,
    KeyWiki.org.

http://keywiki.org/index.php/Barack_Obama_and_the_New_Party/Progressive_Chicago

98. See "October 1996 Update," http://web.archive.org/web/20010306031216/www.newparty.org/up9610.html

99. Editorial, Progressive Populist, November, 1996. http://www.populist.com/11.96.Edit.html

100. "The Truth About Barack Obama and the New Party," FighttheSmears.com, See at http://web.archive.org/web/20090730002941/http://www.fightthesmears.com/articles/28/KurtzSmears.html

101. Stanley Kurtz, "Obama's Third-Party History," NationalReview.com, June 7, 2012. http://www.nationalreview.com/articles/302031/obamas-third-party-history-stanley-kurtz?pg=1

102. Transcript, "McCain, Obama go head to head in last debate," CNN.com, October 19, 2008. http://articles.cnn.com/2008-10-19/politics/ct. presidentialdebate3.transcript_1_tax-cuts-schieffer-of-cbs-news-commission-on-presidential-debates/15?_s=PM:POLITICS

103. Aaron Klein, "Obama website lies about ACORN ties," WorldNetDaily.com, October 12, 2008. http://www.wnd.com/2008/10/77813/

104. "The Lies Politicians Tell," FoxNews.com, February 24, 2010. http://www.foxnews.com/story/0,2933,587286,00.html

105 Association Of Community Organizations For Reform Now (Acorn) http://www.discoverthenetworks.org/groupProfile.asp?grpid=6968

106. Matthew Vadum, "ACORN: Who Funds the Weather Underground's Little Brother?" Foundation Watch, Capital Research Center, November 2008. https://www.capitalresearch.org/pubs/pdf/v1225222922.pdf

107. Kurtz, Stanley (2010-10-19). Radical-in-Chief (p. 192). Simon & Schuster, Inc.. Kindle Edition.

108. Ibid.

109. Ibid.

110. Carey Rogers, "Neighborhood Organizing Leads to Nat'l Platform," Democratic Left, January 1980, p. 9. Quoted in Kurtz, Stanley (2010-10-19). Radical-in-Chief (p. 431). Simon & Schuster, Inc.. Kindle Edition. Kurtz, Stanley (2010-10-19). Radical-in-Chief (p. 39). Simon & Schuster, Inc.. Kindle Edition.

111. Webb Smedley, "Report on the ACORN Convention," NAM Discussion Bulletin, #26, Spring 1979, p. 107. Quoted in Kurtz, Stanley (2010-10-19). Radical-in-Chief (p. 201). Simon & Schuster, Inc.. Kindle Edition.

112. Keith Kelleher, "Growth of a Modern Union Local: A People's History of SEIU Local 880," Just Labour: A Canadian Journal of Work and Society 12 (Spring

2008), http:// www.docstoc.com/ docs/ 11484473/ Obamas-Ties-to-Chicago-SEIU-Local-880-ACORN-Project-VOTE! Quoted in Klein, Aaron; Elliott, Brenda J. (2010-03-05). The Manchurian President (p. 113). Midpoint Trade Books. Kindle Edition.

113. Hank DeZutter, "What Makes Obama Run?" Chicago Reader, December 7, 1995. http://www.chicagoreader.com/chicago/what-makes-obama-run/Content?oid=889221

114. Kurtz, Stanley (2010-10-19). Radical-in-Chief (p. 285). Simon & Schuster, Inc.. Kindle Edition.

115. Klein, Aaron; Elliott, Brenda J. (2010-03-05). The Manchurian President (p. 118). Midpoint Trade Books. Kindle Edition.

116. Ibid., pp. 118-119.

117. Toni Foulkes, "Case Study: Chicago— The Barack Obama Campaign," Social Policy, Winter 2003/ Spring 2004. See at http://www.discoverthenetworks.org/Articles/Chicago%20The%20Barack%20Obama%20Campaign.html

118. Obama, Barack (2007-01-09). Dreams from My Father: A Story of Race and Inheritance (Kindle Locations 5015-5019). Random House, Inc.. Kindle Edition.

119. Cathleen Falsani, "Barack Obama and The God Factor Interview," Sojourners, February 21, 2012, http://sojo.net/blogs/2012/02/21/transcript-barack-obama-and-god-factor-interview 02-21-2012, 3:20pm

120. Stephen Spruiell , "That Rolling Stone Article…," NationalReview.com, April 16, 2008.

121. Jeremiah Wright Controversy, http://en.wikipedia.org/wiki/Jeremiah_Wright_controversy

122. Larry Elder, "Why Jeremiah Wright Matters—Still, Part II," Frontpagemag.org, May 31, 2012. http://frontpagemag.com/2012/larry-elder/why-jeremiah-wright-matters-still-part-ii/

123. "Something Wasn't Wright, Why Oprah Winfrey left Rev. Jeremiah Wright's church," The Daily Beast, May 3, 2008. http://www.thedailybeast.com/newsweek/2008/05/03/something-wasn-t-wright.html

124. Senator Obama on Fox News, http://www.youtube.com/watch?v=79JbkOG31sA&feature=player_embedded

125. Stanley Kurtz, Radical-in-Chief (New York: Simon & Schuster, 2010), 303.

126. William Hordern, "Dialogue on Black Theology, An Interview with James Cone," Chicken Bones: A Journal, http://www.nathanielturner.com/dialogueon-blacktheology.htm

127. James Cone, DiscovertheNetworks.org, http://www.discoverthenetworks.org/individualProfile.asp?indid=2315

128. Ibid.

129. Cone, Black Theology and Black Power, p. 3. Quoted in Kurtz, Stanley (2010-10-19). Radical-in-Chief (p. 301). Simon & Schuster, Inc.. Kindle Edition.

130. James H. Cone, A Black Theology of Liberation (Lippincott, 1970), p. 132. Quoted in James Cone, DiscovertheNetworks.org, http://www.discover-thenetworks.org/individualProfile.asp?indid=2315

131. James H. Cone, My Soul Looks Back (Maryknoll, New York: Orbis Books, [1986] 2005), p. 138. Quoted in Kurtz, Stanley (2010-10-19). Radical-in-Chief (pp. 338-339). Simon & Schuster, Inc.. Kindle Edition.

132. Margaret Talev, "Obama's Church Pushes Contro-versial Doctrines," McClatchy Newspapers, March 20, 2008, http:// www.mcclatchydc.com/ 2008/ 03/ 20/ 31079/ obamas-church-pushes-controversial.html. Cited in Kurtz, Stanley (2010-10-19). Radical-in-Chief (p. 334). Simon & Schuster, Inc.. Kindle Edition.

133. "Obama: Stealth Socialist?" Investor's Business Daily, May 16, 2008. http://news.investors.com/article/466049/200805161445/obama-stealth-socialist-.htm?p=full

134. A Paradoxical Feeling," James Cone interviewed by Hana R. Alberts, Forbes.com, March 24, 2008. http://www.forbes.com/2008/03/24/obama-black-liberation-theology-oped-cx_hra_0324cone.html

135. Stanley Kurtz, Radical-in-Chief (New York: Simon & Schuster, 2010), 301.

136. Humberto Fontova, "Rev. Jeremiah Wright: The Cuban Connection," Frontpage.org, October 15, 2008. http://archive.frontpagemag.com/readArticle.aspx?ARTID=32669

137. Ibid.

138. Cliff Kinkaid, "Controversial New Video of Obama's Pastor," Accuracy in Media, Nov. 1, 2009. http://www.aim.org/aim-column/controversial-new-video-of-obamas-pastor/

139. Jeremiah Wright, DiscovertheNetworks.org, http://www.discoverthenetworks.org/individualProfile.asp?ind id=2307#ref6

140. Kurtz, Stanley (2010-10-19). Radical-in-Chief (p. 341). Simon & Schuster, Inc.. Kindle Edition.

141. "Obama: Stealth Socialist?" Investor's Business Daily, May 16, 2008. http://news.investors.com/article/466049/200805161445/obama-stealth-socialist-.htm?p=full

142. Sasha Abramsky, Inside Obama's Brain (New York: Penguin, 2009), p. 264. Quoted in Kurtz, Stanley

(2010-10-19). Radical-in-Chief (p. 303). Simon & Schuster, Inc.. Kindle Edition.

143. Margaret Talev, "Obama's church pushes controversial doctrines," McClatchy Newspapers, March 20, 2008. http://www.mcclatchydc.com/2008/03/20/31079/oba mas-church-pushes-controversial.html#storylink=cpy

144. Kurtz, Stanley. Radical-in-Chief (Simon & Schuster, Inc., 2010), 253.

145. Ray Long, Ray Gibson, and David Jackson, "State pork to Obama's district included allies, donors," Chicago Tribune, May 3, 2007. http://www.chicagotribune.com/news/nationworld/chi-0705030035may03,0,3860794.story

146. "Obama Says That Pfleger Is A Moral Compass For Him," RedState.com, http://archive.redstate.com/ blogs/wsjreader/2008/may/29/obama_says_that_pflege r_is_a_moral_compass_for_him

147. http://sojo.net/blogs/2012/02/21/transcript-barack-obama-and-god-factor-interview

148. Klein, Edward (2012-05-14). The Amateur (p. 261). Perseus Books Group. Kindle Edition.

149. Michael Pfleger, DiscovertheNetworks.org, http://www. discoverthenetworks.org/individualProfile.asp?indid=2313

150 Ken Dilanian, "Priest who ridiculed Clinton backed Obama," USA Today, May 30, 2008. http://www. usatoday.com/news/politics/election2008/2008-05-30-pfleger_N.htm

151. Jeff Zeleny, "Obama 'Disappointed' by Pastor's Remarks That Were Critical of Clinton," New York Times, May 29, 2008. http://thecaucus.blogs. nytimes.com/2008/05/29/obama-apologizes-for-another-pastor-critical-of-clinton/

152. Michael Pfleger, DiscovertheNetworks.org, http://www. discoverthenetworks.org/individualProfile.asp?indid=2313

153. Michelle Malkin, "Pfleger: "America is the greatest sin against God;" new "statement" to come?" Michelle-Malkin.com, June 2, 2008. http://michellemalkin. com/2008/06/02/pfleger-america-is-the-greatest-sin-against-god/

154. Charles C. Johnson, Breitbart.com, "The Vetting: Meet Obama's Catholic Mentor, Father Michael Pfleger," April 6, 2012. http://www.breitbart.com/Big-Government/2012/04/06/Obama-Pfleger-The-Vetting

155. Robert McClory, Radical Disciple: Father Pfleger, St. Sabina Church, and the Fight for Social Justice (Chicago: Lawrence Hill Books, 2010), p. 157.

156. Bragg, William Washington (2011-09-07). Obama's Radical Roots: Saul Alinsky, Jeremiah Wright, and the Others who Shaped his Worldview (Kindle Locations

1549-1551). Jefferson Adams Library of American History. Kindle Edition.

157. Michael Pfleger, DiscovertheNetworks.org, http://www.discoverthenetworks.org/individualProfile.asp?indid=2313

158. Michael Pfleger, DiscovertheNetworks.org, http://www.discoverthenetworks.org/individualProfile.asp?indid=2313

159. Don Terry, "Farrakhan: Fiery Separatist in a Sober Suit," New York Times, March 3, 1994. http://www.nytimes.com/1994/03/03/us/farrakhan-fiery-separatist-in-a-sober-suit.html?pagewanted=all&src=pm

160. Louis Farrakhan, DiscovertheNetworks.org, http://www.discoverthenetworks.org/individualProfile.asp?indid=1325

161. Michael Pfleger, DiscovertheNetworks.org, http://www.discoverthenetworks.org/individualProfile.asp?indid=2313

162. Don Terry, "Farrakhan: Fiery Separatist in a Sober Suit," New York Times, March 03, 1994. http://www.nytimes.com/1994/03/03/us/farrakhan-fiery-separatist-in-a-sober-suit.html?pagewanted=all&src=pm

163. "Farrakhan Again Describes Hitler as a 'Very Great Man' New York Times, July 17, 1984. http://www.nytimes.com/1984/07/17/us/farrakhan-again-describes-hitler-as-a-very-great-man.html

164. Askia Muhammad, "Farrakhan addresses world at Saviours' Day 2008," The Final Call, March 5, 2008. http://www.finalcall.com/artman/publish/National_News_2/Farrakhan_addresses_world_at_Saviours_Day_2008_4427.shtml

165. Richard Cohen, "Obama's Farrakhan Test," Washington Post, January 14, 2008. http://www.washingtonpost.com/wp-dyn/content/article/2008/01/14/AR2008011402083.html?hpid=opinionsbox1

166. "Russert persisted in questioning Obama on Farrakhan — even after his repeated "denunciation[s]" of Farrakhan's "unacceptable and reprehensible" comments," Media Matters for America, February 27, 2008. http://mediamatters.org/research/200802270006

167. Bragg, William Washington (2011-09-07). Obama's Radical Roots: Saul Alinsky, Jeremiah Wright, and the Others who Shaped his Worldview (Kindle Locations 1761-1762). Jefferson Adams Library of American History. Kindle Edition.

168. "Farrakhan In His Own Words RULE On Jews," Anti-Defamation League. http://www.adl.org/special_reports/farrakhan_own_words2/on_jews.asp

169. Louis Farrakhan, DiscovertheNetworks.org. http://www.discoverthenetworks.org/individualProfile.asp?indid=1325

170. Ibid.

171. Ibid.

172. Ibid.

173. Ibid.

174. Hank DeZutter, "What Makes Obama Run?" The Chicago Reader, December 7, 1995. http://www.chicagoreader.com/chicago/what-makes-obama-run/Content?oid=889221

175. Ibid.

176. Ken Timmerman, "Obama-Farrakhan Ties Are Close, Ex-Aide Says," NewsMax.com, November 2, 2008. http://www.newsmax.com/InsideCover/farrakhan-obama-islam/2008/11/03/id/326298

177. Klein, Aaron; Elliott, Brenda J. (2010-03-05). The Manchurian President (p. 96). Midpoint Trade Books. Kindle Edition.

178. Ibid.

179. Seth Gitell, "Al Sharpton for president?" Boston Phoenix, February 28 - March 7, 2002. http://www.bostonphoenix.com/boston/news_features/top/features/documents/02179033.htm

180. Robert M. Annis, "Ogletree Defends West's Political Involvement," The Crimson, January 11, 2002. http://www.thecrimson.com/article/2002/1/11/ogletree-defends-wests-political-involvement-a/

181. "Former Black Panthers considered terrorists under Patriot Act," It's About Times, December 28, 2005. http://www.itsabouttimebpp.com/Announcements/Former_Black_Panthers.html

182. Jenée Desmond-Harris, "The Man Who Mentored the President," The Root, March 15, 2012. http://www.theroot.com/views/man-who-mentored-president?page=0,1

183. Derrick Bell, DiscovertheNetworks.org. http://www.discoverthenetworks.org/individualProfile.asp?indid=2175

184. Ben Shapiro, "OBAMA: 'Open up your hearts and your minds' to racialist prof," Breitbart.com, March 7, 2012. http://www.breitbart.com/Big-Government/2012/03/07/buzzefeed-selectively-edits-obama-tape/

185. Derrick Bell, DiscovertheNetworks.com, http://www.discoverthenetworks.org/individualProfile.asp?indid=2175

186. Joe Kovacs, "Smoking Gun in Breitbart Mystery Video," WND.com, March 7, 2012. http://www.wnd.com/2012/03/breitbarts-mystery-tapes-on-obama-released/

187. Peter Wallsten, "Allies of Palestinians see a friend in Obama," Los Angeles Times, April 10, 2008.

http://articles.latimes.com/2008/apr/10/nation/na-obamamideast10

188. Andrew C. McCarthy, "The L.A. Times Suppresses Obama's Khalidi Bash Tape, NationalReview.com, October 27, 2008. http://www.nationalreview.com/articles/226104/i-l-times-i-suppresses-obamas-khalidi-bash-tape/andrew-c-mccarthy

189. Ibid.

190. Ibid.

191. Aaron Klein, "Obama worked with terrorists," WorldNetDaily.com, February 24, 2008. http://www.wnd.com/2008/02/57231/

192. Aaron Klein, "Another day, another terror tie for Obama. Professor friend has long historywithArafat's PLO," WorldNetDaily, October 30, 2008, http://www.wnd.com/ index.php? pageId = 79568. Quoted in Klein, Aaron; Elliott, Brenda J. (2010-03-05). The Manchurian President (pp. 47-48). Midpoint Trade Books. Kindle Edition.

193. Rashid Khalidi, DiscovertheNetworks.org, http://www.discoverthenetworks.org/individualProfile.asp?indid=1347

194. Klein, Aaron; Elliott, Brenda J. (2010-03-05). The Manchurian President (p. 48). Midpoint Trade Books. Kindle Edition.

195. "The Klein Example," New York Sun, February 18, 2005. http://www.nysun.com/editorials/klein-example/9477/

196. Aaron Klein, "Obama worked with terrorists," WorldNetDaily.com, February 24, 2008. http://www.wnd.com/2008/02/57231/

197. Klein, Edward (2012-05-14). The Amateur (pp. 107-108). Perseus Books Group. Kindle Edition.

198. Michelle Obama, DiscovertheNetworks.org, http://www.discoverthenetworks.org/individualProfile.asp?indid=2311

199. Klein, Edward (2012-05-14). The Amateur (pp. 107-108). Perseus Books Group. Kindle Edition.

200. Charles Ogletree, KeyWiki.org. http://keywiki.org/index.php/Charles_Ogletree

201. Lauren Collins, "The Other Obama, The New Yorker, March 10, 2008. http://www.newyorker.com/reporting/2008/03/10/080310fa_fact_collins?currentPage=all

202. Michelle Obama, DiscovertheNetworks.org, http://www.discoverthenetworks.org/individualProfile.asp?indid=2311

203. Ibid.

204. Tiffany Gabbay, "'Race Wars' Part 1: The Shocking Data on Black-on-Black Crime," April 9, 2012. ahttp://www.theblaze.com/stories/race-wars-part-1-the-shocking-data-on-black-on-black-crime/

205. Ibid.

206. Kurtz, Stanley (2010-10-19). Radical-in-Chief (p. 184). Simon & Schuster, Inc.. Kindle Edition.

207. Kurtz, Stanley (2010-10-19). Radical-in-Chief (p. 11). Simon & Schuster, Inc.. Kindle Edition.

208. Kurtz, Stanley (2010-10-19). Radical-in-Chief (p. 210). Simon & Schuster, Inc.. Kindle Edition.

209. "NOI PMCC: Heather Booth, Non Profits and Advocacy," New Organizing Institute, February 26, 2009. Video of Heather Booth presentation at http://www.youtube.com/watch?v=Q0m1hhivauY&feature=player_embedded

210. Heather Booth, DiscovertheNetworks.org, http://www.discoverthenetworks.org/individualProfile.asp?indid=1641

211. Kurtz, Stanley (2010-10-19). Radical-in-Chief (p. 136). Simon & Schuster, Inc.. Kindle Edition.

212. Flier for Socialist Feminist Conference, Summer 1975, and Heather Booth, "Outline for Presentation to Community Organizing Workshop," in Midwest Academy Records, Box 253, Folder 6. Quoted in Kurtz, Stanley (2010-10-19). Radical-in-Chief (p. 420). Simon & Schuster, Inc.. Kindle Edition.

213. A correspondent in Washington, D.C., "Committee of Correspondence #2," p. 5, in Midwest Academy Records, Box 3, Folder: Committee of Correspondence 1977. Kurtz, Stanley (2010-10-19). Radical-in-Chief (p. 421). Simon & Schuster, Inc.. Kindle Edition. Kurtz, Stanley (2010-10-19). Radical-in-Chief (p. 151). Simon & Schuster, Inc.. Kindle Edition.

214. Kurtz, Stanley (2010-10-19). Radical-in-Chief (pp. 174-175). Simon & Schuster, Inc.. Kindle Edition.

215. Ibid., p. 171

216. Ibid., p. 163

217. David Moberg, "Obama's Third Way," Shelterforce Online, Spring 2007d, at http:// www.nhi.org/ online/ issues /149/ obama.html; Trevor Loudon, "Obama File 26: William McNary, Yet Another Obama Radical?" September 2, 2008, at http:// newzeal.blogspot.com/ 2008/ 09/ obama -file-26-william-mcnary-yet.html; Abramsky, Inside Obama's Brain, p. 31. Cited in Kurtz, Stanley (2010-10-19). Radical-in-Chief (pp. 172-173). Simon & Schuster, Inc.. Kindle Edition.

218. David Moberg, "Obama's Third Way," Shelterforce Online, Spring 2007, National Housing Institute. http://nhi.org/online/issues/149/obama.html

219. Kurtz, Radical-in-Chief, pp. 154, 166.

220. Interview, David Axelrod, Frontline, June 20, 2008.

http://www.pbs.org/wgbh/pages/frontline/choice2008/interviews/axelrod.html

221. Jeff Zeleny, "Long by Obama's Side, an Adviser Fills a Role That Exceeds His Title," New York Times, October 26, 2008. http://www.nytimes.com/2008/10/27/us/politics/27axelrod.html?_r=2

222. David Axelrod, KeyWiki.org. http://keywiki.org/index.php/David_Axelrod

223. Ibid.

224. "My family has been outed – we're dam Commies – but we ain't paid to be," Marc's Voice. Quoted in Klein, Aaron; Elliott, Brenda J. (2010-03-05). The Manchurian President (pp. 162-163). Midpoint Trade Books. Kindle Edition.

225. Don Rose, KeyWiki.com, http://keywiki.org/index.php/Don_Rose#cite_note-15

226. Ibid.

227. Paul Kengor, "David Axelrod, Lefty Lumberjack," American Spectator, March 2012. http://spectator.org/archives/2012/03/09/david-axelrod-lefty-lumberjack/print

228. David Canter, KeyWiki.com, http://keywiki.org/index.php/David_Canter.

229. Ibid.

230. Klein, Aaron; Elliott, Brenda J. (2010-03-05). The Manchurian President (p. 164). Midpoint Trade Books. Kindle Edition.

231. Ibid., p. 165.

232. Ibid.

233. Paul Kengor, "David Axelrod, Lefty Lumberjack," American Spectator, March 2012. http://spectator.org/archives/2012/03/09/david-axelrod-lefty-lumberjack/print

234. "The Chicago Socialists; A Denial Of The Reports That A Violent Outbreak Would Occur On The Fourth," New York Times, July 3, 1879. http://query.nytimes.com/mem/archive-free/pdf?res=9507E0D91E3FE63BBC4B53DFB1668382669FDE

235. "Four Thousand Armed Men Drilling Nightly – A Secret Agent Sent to New-York," New York Times, April 25, 1878. http://query.nytimes.com/mem/archive-free/pdf?res=9D06E1DB113AE63BBC4D51DFB2668383669FDE

236. "Communism in Chicago," New York Times, April 21, 1879. http://query.nytimes.com/mem/archive-free/pdf?res=9801E7D6123EE63BBC4951DFB2668382669FDE

237. Harold D. Lasswell and Dorothy Blumenstock, World Revolutionary Propaganda: A Chicago Study, (New York: Alfred A. Knopf, 1939), p. 217.

238. Paul Kengor, "David Axelrod, Lefty Lumberjack," The American Spectator, March 2012. http://spectator.org/archives/2012/03/09/david-axelrod-lefty-lumberjack/print

239. Jo Becker and Christopher Drew, "Pragmatic Politics, Forged on the South Side," New York Times, May 11, 2008. http://www.nytimes.com/2008/05/11/us/politics/11chicago.html?pagewanted=print

240. Laura S. Washington, "The Whole World Was Watching," In These Times, August 23, 2008. http://www.inthesetimes.com/article/continued/3876/the_whole_world_was_watching/

Notes

Special Free Offer!

=======================

Two Tea Party Key Tags When You Stand Against The Left's Attacks

Take a personal stand against the Left's attacks on the Tea Party and Grassfire Nation will send you two "Don't Tread On Me" key tags as our free gift—one to keep and one to share.

The front features the "Don't Tread On Me" flag which has become the symbol of our movement while the reverse boldly states, "I Am The Tea Party."

Limit one set per citizen. Offer good only to patriotic citizens who uphold the Tea Party values of Liberty and Limited Government — and while supplies last.

Visit Grassfire.com/freekeytag to request your gifts.

Spread The Word By Ordering *Team Obama* In Bulk!

___$_____ (any amount) for 2 COPIES

___$30 for 10 COPIES

___$45 for 20 COPIES

___$95 for 50 COPIES

___$150 for 150 COPIES

_____

First Name   *Last Name*

_____

Street Address

_____

City   *State*   *Zip*

(Order form on back)

Call 866-GRASSFIRE or visit
Grassfire.com/TeamObama to order, you may also mail
your check (payable to "Grassfire") to:
Grassfire Nation, PO Box 277, Maxwell, IA 50161

Please charge my credit card:

☐ MasterCard   ☐ VISA   ☐ AMEX   ☐ Discover

Card #:_____

Expiration Date: ___/___ Amount: $_____

Print name (as it appears on card):

_____

Authorized Signature (REQUIRED):

_____

Today's Date: _____

69 Obama Lies

He was hailed as a transformational figure who would usher in a new age of hope and healing to the American political landscape... But even before taking office, the reality that is Barack Hussein Obama has been marked by a dizzying array of lies and distortions that continue tearing at the very fabric of our nation...

Answering the call to chronicle and detail Obama's Lies, Grassfire Nation's researchers have compiled a chilling 122-page resource highlighting the dangerous and dishonest nature that is Obama...

   ___$_____ (any amount) for 2 COPIES

   ___$30 for 10 COPIES

   ___$45 for 20 COPIES

   ___$95 for 50 COPIES

   ___$150 for 150 COPIES

(Order form on back)

Call 866-GRASSFIRE or visit
Grassfire.com/69LiesBulk to order, you may also mail
your check (payable to "Grassfire") to:
Grassfire Nation, PO Box 277, Maxwell, IA 50161

_____

First Name   *Last Name*

_____

Street Address

_____

City   *State*   *Zip*

Please charge my credit card:

☐ MasterCard   ☐ VISA   ☐ AMEX   ☐ Discover

Card #:_____

Expiration Date: ___/___ Amount: $_____

Print name (as it appears on card):

_____

Authorized Signature (REQUIRED):

_____

Today's Date: _____

Get The "Tea Party Survival Guide"!

To survive and overcome the Left's blistering Anti-Tea Party strategy, Grassfire Nation's researchers have assembled the 2012 Tea Party Survival Guide — a pocket-sized powerhouse containing more than 140 pages of critical information and insight on what to expect and how to respond in the critical months ahead.

We've also included the U.S. Constitution and Declaration of Independence — all of which will empower you during this vital election season. Complete the form below to order your Survival Guides or call 866-GRASSFIRE.

     ___$_____ (any amount) for 2 COPIES

     ___$25 for 10 COPIES

     ___$45 for 20 COPIES

     ___$95 for 50 COPIES

     ___$150 for 150 COPIES

(Order form on back)

Call 866-GRASSFIRE or visit Grassfire.com/BulkSur-
vivalGuide to order, you may also mail your
check (payable to "Grassfire") to:
Grassfire Nation, PO Box 277, Maxwell, IA 50161

_____

First Name   *Last Name*

_____

Street Address

_____

City   *State*   *Zip*

Please charge my credit card:

MasterCard   VISA   AMEX   Discover

Card #:_____

Expiration Date: ___/___ Amount: $_____

Print name (as it appears on card):

_____

Authorized Signature (REQUIRED):

_____

Today's Date: _____

SEE OBAMA STRIPPED BARE. (HIS AGENDA, THAT IS.)

Obama Exposed is the blockbuster resource that lays out the 21 ways that Barack Obama has radically re-shaped America into his own image. In 64 compelling pages, you'll see how the son of Kenyan Muslim and a liberal socialist is implementing the most leftist political agenda our nation has ever seen.

Obama Exposed outlines the 21 ways Obama's worldview and policies are impacting your life, your family and our nation. And it's the perfect companion to 69 Lies. Complete the form below or call 866-GRASSFIRE.

> __$10 for 2 COPIES.
>
> __$20 for TE10N COPIES
>
> __$50 for 50 COPIES
>
> __$75 for 100 COPIES
>
> (Order form on back)

Call 866-GRASSFIRE or visit Grassfire.com/ObamaExposedBulk to order, you may also mail your check (payable to "Grassfire") to:
Grassfire Nation, PO Box 277, Maxwell, IA 50161

_____

First Name   Last Name

_____

Street Address

_____

City   State   Zip

Please charge my credit card:

☐ MasterCard   ☐ VISA   ☐ AMEX   ☐ Discover

Card #:_____

Expiration Date: ___/___ Amount: $_____

Print name (as it appears on card):

_____

Authorized Signature (REQUIRED):

_____

Today's Date: _____

Get "Tea"-Filtered News That Tells The Real Story...

Let's face it... the Liberal media has an agenda... an anti-conservative, anti-Tea Party agenda that props up the statist attack on our liberties. That's why Grassfire launched its own news network — LibertyNews.com. Liberty News is news by and from a Tea Party/patriot perspective. That's because all of our researchers, reporters and bloggers are Tea Party faithful.

Visit LibertyNews.com today and start getting your news, tea-filtered.

Where More Tea Party Citizens Gather Every Day...

Every day, tens of thousands of Tea Party citizens come together at PatriotActionNework.com to chat, share, discuss, organize and strategize. One of the nation's fastest growing conservative social action networks, "PAN," offers all the social networking tools you'll find on Facebook in a forum that's just for us.

Launch your own full-service blog. Manage your home page and profile. Join online chats with other Conservatives. Post in dozens of forums. Join your state group. And that's just for starters. With hundreds of thousands of visitors every month, PAN is quickly becoming the online hub for Tea Party conservatives.

Go to PatriotActionNetwork and open your account today!